KT-407-928

CONVEYANCING

A Practical Guide

Revised Edition

Peter Wade

Emerald Guides

www.straightforwardco.co.uk

X400 000006 8384

Emerald Guides

© Revised Edition Peter Wade Estate 2020

All rights reserved. No part of this publication may be reproduced in a retrieval system or transmitted by any means, electronic or mechanical, photocopying or otherwise, without the prior permission of the copyright holders.

ISBN: 978-1-913342-81-4

Printed by 4edge Ltd www.4edge.co.uk

Cover design by BW Studios Derby

Whilst every effort has been made to ensure that the information contained within this book is correct at the time of going to press, the author and publisher can take no responsibility for the errors or omissions contained within.

Wolverhampton City Council	
X400 000006 8384	
Askews & Holts	18-Jan-2021
	£9.99
	1CL

CONVEYANCING-A PRACTICAL GUIDE

Contents

*

This book, updated to **2020**, is not a substitute for a qualified professional and is not presented as such. The information contained within is for use as guidance and at all times the advice of professionals should be sought, as only the extremely confident and experienced lay person, or actual practitioner can buy or sell property alone. In addition, if a mortgage is involved, the lender will insist on a qualified conveyancer.

Risks of DIY Conveyancing

Mistakes made during conveyancing transactions can be Celatively trivial, for example carrying out the wrong search and having to pay a search fee twice, or extremely serious, for example misinterpreting a search result and buying an un-saleable property or finding that following completion it is not possible to register the transaction. When acting in a sale, failure to understand your obligations and responsibilities can lead to giving information for which the buyer can later sue, or being conned by the buyer into parting with money or reducing the price.

So, as stated above, usually when buying or selling residential property, solicitors or licensed conveyancers are normally used in order to ensure that the transaction proceeds smoothly. Both are regulated professionals whose governing bodies require that they be insured and properly regulated. Licensed conveyancers are regulated by the Council of Licensed Conveyancers, solicitors by the Solicitors Regulation Authority or Law Society. Both carry out the process of buying and selling property in a similar way. There are several legal differences between the professions. Conveyancers are allowed to represent both buyer and seller, whereas solicitors generally don't because of conflict of interest.

Similarly, licensed conveyancers need not tell their client if they have received a commission from a marketing or referral agency, whereas solicitors must disclose such commissions. In general, licensed conveyancers may be more suited to a lower value or uncomplicated sale-and it will be much cheaper. If the sale is complex and expensive then a solicitor will be better suited.

Another development in 2019 is that new rules for conveyancers are now in place in Britain aimed at helping home buyers make a more informed choice when buying a property.

All property lawyers must now publish price, service and quality information on their websites, or in alternative formats if requested, as part of a cross-industry push to empower consumers and foster innovation and competition across the legal services market.

The Council for Licensed Conveyancers (CLC) said that all property lawyers will now have to display certain information including costs and provide examples of their fees that cover a broad range of services and transaction types.

This might include information on conveyancing timescales and links to third party feedback platforms and a buyer should be able to easily identify who regulates the firm. For lawyers regulated by the CLC, this includes displaying the CLC secure badge in a prominent place.

All lawyers need to display details of their complaints process including access to the Legal Ombudsman and redress information and while lawyers do not need to disclose specific details of referral arrangements on their website, they must say if they enter into such agreements and the average fee, or range of fees, they pay.

However, notwithstanding the above. the actual processes of conveyancing are usually a mystery to both buyer and seller who are not privy to the procedures. The aim of this brief but concise book is to throw some light on the basic processes, thus ensuring that those who are involved at least have some understanding of what is happening and can question those acting for them at any given point. The book should be read in conjunction with "A Straightforward Guide to Buying and Selling Property" which deals with the more general aspects such as the involvement of estate agents.

Although it is safe to say that the average basic conveyance of a leasehold flat or freehold house is relatively simple and unproblematic, there are still fundamental ground rules which one must observe. When purchasing a leasehold flat for example, particularly in a multi-occupied block, the lease has to be very closely scrutinised and all the covenants in the lease understood. Leases can be unintelligible documents, couched in redundant language, badly laid out and misleading at the best of times.

Leases contain landlord and tenants covenants, which impose rights and obligations on the respective parties, particularly in relation to repairing obligations and service charge and ground rent payments. Other covenants may impose an onerous burden on the leaseholder and quite often only an experienced eye can pick this up. Likewise, the Freehold transfer document may contain obligations, which can only be picked up or understood, by an experienced eye.

Therefore, even if you decide to carry out conveyancing yourself you should always get a sound second opinion concerning the lease or freehold document.

What about online conveyancing?

Traditionally, homebuyers have used local solicitors or conveyancers, often recommended by their estate agent or mortgage lender. However, online conveyancing is a growing area that is transforming the industry – generally for the better.

Online conveyancing companies sell their services over the web, usually backed up by a call centre. They are often based in business parks and are effectively warehouses of fully trained conveyancers dealing with thousands of property transactions. They are usually much more efficient and better value as a result of economies of scale and not being based in city centres. Like ordinary solicitors, the quality of service can be mixed. You deal with them via email and telephone and never see them face to face. Some online conveyancers' business models means your file is on a system and you talk to different people each time.

This can be frustrating. Others allocate your file to one person which provides you with a point of contract.

Good online conveyancers should enable you to access your file 24/7, so you can see its progress. This is useful because when sellers badger buyers for updates you can tell them immediately. Be aware that many websites describe themselves as online conveyancing, but are actually just price comparison websites which will get quotes for you from third party conveyancers or solicitors. This can be very helpful in finding a cheap service, but you can't be sure about sort of quality of service you are going to get from whoever you end up with. However, conveyancers –

whether online or not – cannot deal with complex legal issues, and you should then go with a solicitor.

COVID 19 and the Conveyancing process

The onset of the pandemic and the general lockdown in Mar4ch 2020 caused many problems within the housing market, affecting all involved, not least conveyancers. Although, at the time of writing, November 2020, we have another lockdown, the situation with conveyancing transactions has eased up and things are getting back to as normal a state as they can do. However, the Law Society issued the below statement to help clarify matters which have arisen (bear in mind this advice is for the legal profession and relates largely to contractual matters):

'Queries about the impact of the coronavirus on conveyancing transactions have prompted the Law Society to issue guidance.

'Focus on the impact of the Covid-19 pandemic has so far heavily centred on the retail and hospitality industries. However, the Society said it has received many questions from members on residential conveyancing transactions.

Potential issues raised include: requests for properties to be decontaminated; refusal to vacate on completion because the seller is in self-isolation; banking system disruption, such as CHAPS; removal companies being reluctant to enter properties; and difficulties obtaining witnesses or physical survey valuations.

Before exchange, the Society says there is unlikely to be any drafting solution that would be appropriate to every case. 'You should review your existing contracts and test what the position would be in certain situations on the basis of that contract,' the Society says.

Your client may wish you to negotiate new provisions to suit particular circumstances. We do not consider that bespoke clauses are necessary or desirable as standard.
Once you've assessed the contract that you're proposing to use, you'll be in a better position to establish if any additional provisions are required or desirable in the particular circumstances of the transaction that is, or may be, affected.'

Chancery Lane says there is a difference between transactions where Covid-19 is present and all other situations where it is a possibility. Exchanging contracts on a 'business as usual' may be preferable to using new provisions but this should be assessed. Should completion not take place after contracts have been exchanged due to the virus, the Society says the parties not completing will be in default.

It says: 'The contract provisions relating to default will apply unless the non-defaulting party takes a "good faith" view. If the transaction forms part of a chain of transactions, it may not be possible to take such a view without incurring a penalty.'
For further updated guidance go to:

www.lawgazette.co.uk/news/coronavirus

As we will see later, there are two forms of conveyancing in existence, registered and unregistered. The former means that the ownership of land and all that entails, including extent of ownership, is registered at the Land Registry. The very fact of registration ensures that legal title can be verified. Unregistered land has to be proven through production of deeds, which can be time consuming and problematic. Land Registration has been compulsory in the United Kingdom for a while now, but it is still a fact that a fairly significant amount of all property is unregistered.

This book details the processes of conveyancing a it affects both registered and unregistered land. It then goes on to deal with the advanced stages of conveyancing as it affects unregistered land and also the process of conveyancing registered land. Following the conclusion, which combines a complete summary of the conveyancing process, is a glossary of terms and a list of useful address. There are appendices, containing sample letters and a summary of conveyancing costs plus sample forms.

**

Ch. 1

Overview of the Stages of Conveyancing of Registered Land

This chapter provides a comprehensive summary of the conveyancing process from start to finish.

Chapters 2-3-4 and 5 outline the processes in more detail when acting for sellers, purchasers and also exchange of contracts plus completion and post-completion.

Brief Outline of a Conveyancing Transaction

A conveyancing transaction breaks down into three stages whether we are dealing with a sale or a purchase:

- The pre-contract stage.
- The time between exchange of contracts and completion or pre-completion stage; and
- Post-completion stage.

The pre-contract stage is the longest and most complicated (contrary to what estate agents might tell you). Most of the legal work is done at this stage. Once contracts are exchanged things become time critical. All of the delays take place up to exchange of contracts and these can be attributable to things such as completing the chain of transactions, local authority searches and time for everyone to obtain their mortgages and organise other finance, such as help- to-buy funding or parental loans. In a chain of transactions obviously the chain only proceeds at the pace of the slowest party.

Key Stages of Conveyancing Explained for Selling & Buying

Whether you are selling or buying a home, it's a good idea to know what is involved, and to understand how the Conveyancing process works. The step by step guide below explains the different stages of the Conveyancing process for a typical property sale and purchase transaction.

Overview of the Conveyancing Process for Selling a Property

1. Seller's Conveyancer (law firm or independent conveyancer) instructed.
2. Seller's Conveyancer confirms instructions by letter setting out the terms of business and fixed fee costs.
3. Seller's Conveyancer carries out proof of identity checks (see appendix 2) and sends out a fittings and contents form and property information form(s) for completion. If the property is leasehold, additional information will be required. See appendix 3 for form.
4. Seller to complete fittings and contents form and property information form(s) (see appendix 3).

5. Seller's Conveyancer obtains title deeds from deeds holder or official copies of the title register and any other documents required by The Land Registry and details of the amount outstanding on any existing mortgage.
6. Seller's Conveyancer prepares the draft contract and supporting contract documentation and sends to the buyer's Conveyancer.
7. Buyer's Conveyancer checks the contract and supporting contract documentation and raises pre-contract enquiries with the seller's Conveyancer.
8. Seller's Conveyancer and seller answer pre-contract enquiries.
9. Buyer's Conveyancer confirms they have acceptable results from their searches, are happy with the answers to pre-contract enquiries and are in receipt of a mortgage offer (if any).
10. Seller and buyer agree on a completion date and contracts are formally "exchanged" - meaning both parties are legally committed to the transaction. Seller's Conveyancer will obtain a settlement figure to repay the outstanding amount on any existing mortgage, if applicable. Buyer's Conveyancer drafts a transfer deed (TR1) and sends to the Seller's Conveyancer.
11. Seller's Conveyancer checks the transfer deed and sends to the seller for signature in readiness for completion.

12. On completion the seller must vacate the property at a time to be agreed and make arrangements to hand over the keys, usually through the estate agent.
13. Buyer's Conveyancer will send the proceeds of sale to the seller's Conveyancer and the seller's Conveyancer will arrange for the keys to be released to the buyer.
14. The seller's Conveyancer sends the title deeds and transfer deed to the buyer's Conveyancer together with an undertaking to use the proceeds of sale to discharge any existing mortgage.
15. The seller's Conveyancer then pays the estate agent (if one was used), repays the amount owing to the existing mortgage lender (if applicable) and takes payment for their Conveyancing service costs.

Once all the payments have been made all the remaining money from the sale will be transferred to the seller, usually by bank transfer on the day of completion.

Overview of the Conveyancing Process for Buying a Property

Buyer makes an offer on the property, which is accepted by the seller.

1. Buyer's Conveyancer instructed on acceptance of the offer.
2. Buyer arranges a survey on the property, and makes an application for a mortgage (if required).
3. Buyer's Conveyancer confirms instructions by letter setting out the terms of business and fixed fee costs.

4. Buyer's Conveyancer contacts the seller's Conveyancer to obtain the contract pack.
5. Buyers Conveyancer checks the contract pack, raises pre-contract enquiries (form TA6) and also sends new home information form (TA8), carries out the necessary searches and obtains a copy of the mortgage offer.
6. Sellers's Conveyancer and seller answer pre-contract enquiries and return these to buyer's Conveyancer.
7. Buyer's Conveyancer reviews and reports to the buyer on the contents of the contract pack, pre-contract enquiries, the result of the searches and mortgage offer. The buyer then considers this report and raises questions on anything that is unclear.
8. When the buyer is happy to proceed, arrangements are made for the deposit to be paid to the buyer's Conveyancer in readiness for exchange of contracts.
9. Seller and buyer agree on a completion date and contracts are formally "exchanged" - meaning both parties are legally committed to the transaction.
10. Buyer's Conveyancer prepares a draft transfer deed and completion information form and sends these to the seller's Conveyancer for completion.
11. Seller's solicitor approves the draft transfer deed and a final copy is made. This may need to be signed by the buyer before being sent to the seller's solicitor for signature by the seller in readiness for completion.

12. Buyer's Conveyancer prepares a completion statement, carries out pre-completion searches and applies to the buyer's mortgage lender for the mortgage loan.
13. On completion, the buyer vacates the property by the agreed time and buyer's Conveyancer sends the proceeds of sale to the seller's Conveyancer.
14. Seller's Conveyancer releases the keys to the estate agent (if one was used) and sends the title deeds and transfer deed to the buyer's Conveyancer together with an undertaking to repay any existing mortgage.
15. Buyer's Conveyancer sends the stamp duty payable to HMRC, receives the title deeds, transfer deed and proof that the seller has paid the outstanding mortgage on the property.
16. Buyer's Conveyancer registers the property in the name of the buyer at The Land Registry.
17. The buyer receives a copy of the registered title from The Land Registry. Any documents required by the mortgage lender to be retained by them are sent on by the Buyer's solicitor.

Having summarised the conveyancing process, through a series of key steps it is now time to look in more detail at the function of the Land Registry and, in Chapter 3, at the processes involved in conveyancing unregistered land.

Ch. 2

The Land Registry

Outline of the Land Registry and the registration process

In registered land the documents of title are replaced by the fact of registration. Therefore, the equivalent to the title deed is the various entries in the Land Registry.

Each title is given a number, which is then used to trace title. The description of each title is identified by a title number, described by reference to a filed plan and a set of index cards retained to record specifics about that title.

The index cards and the filed plan are the equivalent of title deeds. The registered proprietor is issued with a land certificate containing a facsimile copy of the registered title. If land within a particular title number is subject to a mortgage the land certificate is retained by the Registry and the mortgagee is instead issued with a charge certificate.

There are three registers of title at the Land Registry, the Property Register, The Proprietorship Register and the Charges Register.

The Property Register is similar to the Parcel Clause in unregistered conveyancing i.e., it describes the land in question. It will identify the geographical location and extent of the registered property by means of a short description and a reference to an official plan, which is prepared for each title. It may also give particulars of any rights that benefit the land, for example, a right of way over adjoining land. In the case of a lease the register will also describe the parties to the lease, the term and the rent, any exceptions or reservations from the lease and, if the lessors title is registered, the title number.

The Proprietorship Register will describe the type of title, i.e. title absolute, leasehold etc, the full name and address of the registered proprietor, description of that person, date of registration, price paid for the property and any other relevant entries. There will also be any relevant cautions, inhibitions or restrictions entered on the Register.

The Charges Register contains any encumbrance affecting the registered property, such as mortgages and any other charges taken over the property. However, details of the amount of money involved are not disclosed.

How to inspect the Register

The Land Registry has an online conveyancing system. Normally, solicitors use this and evidence of title can be deduced by going into the web site. Evidence of title can also be obtained by visting the Land Registry website at Gov.uk: www.gov.uk/government/organisations/land-registry

For a fee information about title can be obtained. You can also phone the Land Registry Customer Support Team on 0300 006 0411 or email at. : customersupport@landregistry.gsi.gov.uk

The Land/Charge Certificate

Prior to 2003, when a title was registered for the first time or changed hands, a Land Certificate was issued by the Land Registry. The Land Certificate was regarded as the equivalent to the title deed although this can be misleading as it is only a facsimile of the official register and may not be up to date. In addition, there may be matters of title not contained on the register.

As mentioned in the introduction, following the introduction of the Land Registration Act 2002, and the practice of 'Dematerialisation' Land and Charge Certificates have now been abolished. If you have lost your certificate you do not need to replace it. Electronic copies of the land certificate can now be obtained through the Land Registry website.

Maps and descriptions of land

The Index map and parcels index provides that a map should be kept showing the position and extent of all registered titles. This is called the Public Index Map. This is open to inspection by any person, and can be inspected personally or by official search There will be a fee for this search.

All registered land must, in addition, be described by the applicant in such a way as to enable the land to be fully identified on the ordnance map or general map.

The Land Registry uses a consistent colour coding on its plans. This does not vary and it is expected that solicitors when preparing plans will use the same system. The colouring scheme is as follows:

- Red edging marks the extent of land within a particular title.
- Green tinting shows excluded pieces of land within the area of the title.
- Brown tinting shows land over which the registered land has a right of way.
- Blue tinting shows land within the title subject to a right of way.

For further references, colours are used in the following order:

- Tinting in pink, blue yellow and mauve.
- Edging with a blue yellow or mauve band.
- Hatching with a colour other than black or green.
- Numbering or lettering of small self contained areas.

In addition, when reading a filed plan it should be noted that a boundary represented by a feature shown on the ground or on the existing ordnance survey is represented by a continuous dark line. A boundary not representing such a feature is shown by a broken dark line. The scale of the filed plan is usually 1/1250 enlarged from the survey 1/2500.

****

Ch: 3

Unregistered Land-First Registration of a Title

In practice, most property is now registered at the Land Registry. However, there are still a few titles which remain unregistered, such as those properties which have been lived in continuously since before registration became mandatory.

Note:
Practice introduced on 28 November 2016:
Conveyancers can lodge certified copy deeds and documents instead of originals, provided they meet certain conditions.

First Registration
First registration of a title must take place within two months of new triggers (instructions),

The Land Registry have issued practice advice leaflets which contains detailed guidance about unregistered land and the process of registering unregistered titles.

First registrations (PG1)
First Registration if title deeds are lost or destroyed (PG2)
Cautions against first registration (PG3

For further guidance go to:
https://www.gov.uk/government/publications/first-registrations

The only estates capable of registration are freehold and leasehold titles.

All leases over 7 years are registerable leases, and should be registered at the Land Registry.

Classes of Registered Title

Freehold absolute – this is the best class of Title available. The Titleholder will take the legal estate, subject to any encumbrances protected by an entry on the register and overriding interest.

Freehold Possessory – the registrar is not satisfied with the applicant's title, possessory title will be issued. The proprietor will take title subject to any adverse interest, which exist or are capable of existing at the date of the first registration.

Freehold Qualified – this title is very rare. It is for freehold land where there is defect or flaw affecting the applicant's title.

Leasehold Absolute – This is for a term of years equivalent to the freehold absolute class. If an unregistered lease with more than 7 years to run is assigned for value or by gift, it will be the subject of compulsory first registration.

Leasehold Possessory – subject to any estate of interest that is adverse to the proprietor's title at the time of first registration.

Leasehold qualified - the registrar believes that there is a flaw or defect in the leasehold title.

Good leasehold – the registration is such that there is no guarantee that the lease has been invalidly granted, this will be issued when the registrar has not seen the superior title. The problem for this of course is that if the lease is held to be invalid, the lender will lose its security.

****

Ch. 4

More Detailed Information-The Pre-Completion Stage

As we have seen, the most protracted element of the conveyancing process is the pre-completion stage, the time between first instruction and exchange of contracts.. Here, the seller's solicitors must prepare a pre-completion package for the purchaser's solicitors

This consists of:
The draft contract which describes the land that is being sold and the price together with all the other terms of the transaction such as interest rates in the event of late completion, the amount of the deposit etc.

For sample draft contracts covering freehold and leasehold properties, visit

www.freeconveyancingadvice.co.uk/sale-purchase/conveyancing-contracts

Evidence of the seller's title which consists of official office copies of the sellers' title at the land registry together with the filed plan. You can purchase the office copy entries and title plan for a fee on the Land Registry website

www.landregistryservices.com

Fixtures, fittings and contents list and solicitors property information form (see appendix).

It may also include copy planning permissions, building regulations consents and guarantees.

Title

This usually consists of the official copies of the entries at the land registry but still may be unregistered title.

Property Searches

Property searches (also known as conveyancing searches) are enquiries made by a solicitor to find out more information about a property to be purchased. As part of the home-buying process, a conveyancer will carry out a variety of 'searches' with the local authority and other parties.

The main searches when buying a house are:

- Local Authority
- Water and Property
- Environmental

They typically include aspects such as whether planning permission may be granted for a future development that would negatively impact your property, the quality of the ground on which your house is built or details of common drains and access rights.

The conveyancing searches should be completed and approved before you exchange contracts and legally commit yourself to purchasing the property, as they may highlight planning or structural issues that could either affect the value of the property, or result in additional costs further down the line.

How long do Searches take?

There are over 340 local authorities across the UK. Searches are managed differently depending on your local authority so turnaround time can take between 48 hours to several weeks for your search results to be returned. Local searches can vary due to the method in which your local authority return search results. For example, if you receive your search results electronically via an online portal or email this will be much quicker than by post.

Many local authorities only have small teams working in the Land Charges departments, so during busy periods it could take longer for them to return your search results.

Local Authority Searches

A local authority search will provide you with detailed information about your property and the surrounding areas. This will give you peace of mind before going ahead with the purchase of your new home and ensure you avoid any nasty surprises in the future.

There are two parts to a local authority search, a LLC1 result and a CON29 result. These are the forms that you fill in to carry out searches and will be on the Local Authority property searches website. The LLC1 results will tell you the following information about your property:

- If your property is a listed building
- Located in a conservation area
- Situated in a tree preservation order area
- Need an improvement or renovation grant
- In a smoke control area

Any future development plans that could affect your property are assessed by CON29. The CON29 results are broken down into two different parts (required and optional).

The required results will reveal:

- Proposals for new roads or traffic schemes
- Contaminated land
- Planning decisions affecting your property
- Building regulations
- If your property is in a Radon affected area

From time to time additional information may be required using the CON29 form. Examples include, road proposals by private bodies, completion notices, land maintenance notices and environmental and pollution notice. CON29 works to assess any changes that could be made in the near future that may affect your property.

Water, drainage and other property searches

It is also recommended for first time buyers to apply to the local water company responsible for the property asking for confirmation that the sewers, drains and piping are maintained by them. A water and drainage search carried out by your conveyancer will also highlight the proximity of the property to public sewers and whether the property has a sewer running within the boundaries of the property.

Environmental search

An environmental search identifies whether the previous land use of the property creates a potential environmental risk or is risk free. This type of search will highlight issues including:

- Landslips
- Subsidence
- Contaminated land due to historic landfills and waste sites
- The risk of flooding from nearby rivers or seas

In certain cases, a conveyancer may recommend carrying out the following non-routine searches, depending on the location of the property:

Commons registration-If a property borders with common land, a village green or is in a rural area a search is recommended in accordance with the Commons Registration Act 1965. This property search should also be carried out when purchasing agricultural land.

Mining search-A mining search is required if the property is situated in an area of previous or current mining history and is at risk of being built on unstable ground. This search is largely carried out for the benefit of the mortgage lender.

Land charges -This is a search that should be taken when dealing with unregistered land, detailing any bankruptcy proceedings attributed to the owner of the land. It will also highlight if there are any restrictions on the use of land, estate contracts and mortgages.

Chancel repair liability-All parochial church councils in England and Wales were given until October 2013 to identify and register any land bound to chancel repair liability. This information is kept by the Land Registry and stored on the Title Register database, so if you buy or inherit a property and you live within the parishes of the church, it is worth checking if you are liable to contribute towards the cost of repairs to the church.

Disadvantaged area searches

These are relevant to freehold properties costing £150,000 or less.

Nowadays the processes of searching are relatively quick. Once this information has been obtained and the draft contract has been prepared then the path to exchanging contracts can be quite smooth (in theory).

The next two chapters, 5-6 deal with the specific steps taken by conveyancers when acting for the seller and also the purchaser. This is followed in chapters 6-7 by the exchange of contracts, completion and post completion.

****

Ch. 5

Step-By-Step-Acting For The Seller

Having detailed a summary of the conveyancing process from start to finish, plus outlined dealing with unregistered titles and preliminary work, we will now look specifically at the detailed work involved when acting for the seller.

When dealing with the seller, it is of the utmost importance that you should take as detailed instructions as possible at the outset. Constantly asking the client further questions undermines their confidence.

Tax and Planning Consequences

By obtaining full instructions other matters can be taken into account such as:

- Insuring the property
- Inheritance tax
- Co-ownership
- Planning
- Take instructions in person where possible, in a personal interview.
- Co-Sellers

Authority should be obtained from any co-seller or purchaser.

Status of the Conveyancer

The status of the conveyancer should be confirmed to the client and details of the complaints procedure given.

Protocol Forms

When transacting a sale, certain forms, known as protocol forms will be used to elicit information from the seller. (see appendix 3)

- Property Information Form TA6 (4th Edition 2020)
- Fittings and Contents TA10 (3rd Edition)
- Leasehold Information Form TA7 (2nd Edition)

The above are the main forms used. In addition the below may be used depending on the circumstances:

- TA8 New Home Information form
- TA9 Commonhold Information form
- TA13 Completion information and Undertakings

All of the above forms can be purchased from the Law Society bookshop www.lawsociety.org.uk.

They are also available from a number of other outlets detailed on the law society website (detailed overleaf):

- Advanced Legal & Laserform
- LexisNexis
- Easy Convey
- Oyez
- Peapod Legal
- Shaw & Sons Ltd
- Leap
- Infotrack
- ULS Technology

Sellers Checklist-Information required

When selling a property the solicitor should obtain or deduce:

1. Client – full names and addresses of sellers, buyers home and business telephone numbers
2. Estate agents details
3. Where are the Title Deeds?
4. Client's authority to obtain them
5. Full address of the property
6. Price
7. Deposits
8. Fixtures and Fittings-are they being removed?
9. Any instructions on completion date
10. Various use of the premises
11. Who is resident at the premises
12. Is there a chain?
13. Any other special conditions
14. Any tenancy

15. Advice as to Costs
16. Any outstanding mortgages
17. Where the proceeds of sale are to go
18. Any Capital Gains Tax on sale proceeds
19. Does it have to be synchronised with any other related purchase (Chain)
20. Obtain answers to Sellers Property Information Form and Fixtures, Fittings and Contents
21. Check Identity of Client

SALES CONSIDERATIONS

- Request Title Deeds
- Request Office Copy Entries
- Draft Contract.

STANDARD CONDITIONS OF SALE (Fifth Edition)

Standard conditions of the contract normally incorporate the Standard Conditions of Sale 5th edition. This can be obtained from the Law Society's website.

The Seller is to transfer the property with either full title guarantee or limited title guarantee, as specified on the front page of the Contract. Standard conditions of sale set out all aspects of the transaction and formation of the contract:

- Deposit
- Matters affecting the property

- Physical state
- Title and Transfer

Deposit

The buyer is to pay or send a deposit of 10% (usually) of the total of the purchase price and the Chattels price (i.e. furniture, carpets, curtains etc) no later than the date of the contract.

Matters affecting the property

The property is sold free from encumbrances, other than those mentioned in the contract, those discoverable by inspection

Physical State

The Buyer accepts the property in the physical state it is in at the date of the contract unless the seller is building or converting it.

Title and Transfer

The condition sets out how the seller will deduce title to both registered and unregistered land

Requisitions

The buyer may be precluded from raising requisitions on items that have been disclosed prior to exchange of contracts

Commonhold

This is under the Commonhold and Leasehold format 2002.The seller must provide a copy of the memorandum and articles of the common holders association and of the Commonhold community statement. The front page of the contract sets out the sellers and buyers names.

Also a description of the property whether it is freehold or leasehold and its postal address, title number or Root of Title and any specified encumbrances

Title Guarantee – whether full or limited

When it has full title guarantee the seller has the right to dispose of the property and will at their own expense, make every reasonable effort to transfer the title offered, and the seller transfers free of all charges and encumbrances. Limited title guarantee states that the transferor has not himself or herself encumbered the property and is not aware that anyone else has. An example of this would be a personal representative.

In leasehold titles both full and limited title guarantee imply that the lease is subsisting and that there is no existing breach that might result in forfeiture.

A plan is usually necessary for either transfer of whole or transfer of part, obviously more easily obtained now that most properties are registered. It is possible to obtain a plan from the Land Registry by asking on the Index map search and this plan can be agreed for the transfer and the contract.

Sending the papers to the Purchasers Solicitors

- Draft contract in duplicate – you are recommended to keep your own file copy.
- The Protocol forms- Fixtures, Fittings and Contents, and Property Information Form plus any other used, as detailed in appendix 3.
- For Leasehold title, you would normally include Last service charge and three years accounts.
- Copy of Share Certificate of Management Company
- Copy of memorandum and articles of association
- Copy of block insurance policy and schedule
- Any guarantees, damp, timber, preservation etc
- Any copy of planning permission as building regulation consent
- Further enquiries from purchaser's solicitors.

It is recommended that you take the client's express instructions concerning any replies to further enquiries.
The client will be liable for any misrepresentation in giving the reply.

If there has been any breach of planning or building regulation consent it is possible to obtain an indemnity.

Receiving Draft Contract

Report to client on contract and obtain their execution thereto
Confirm price, chattels, rates of interest etc with client.

If appropriate obtain client's instructions concerning a date for completion.

The TR1

This is the Formal land registry document prepared by conveyancers and transfers property from seller to buyer. It needs to be agreed by both parties and then signed by the seller before completion can take place. It is usually signed between exchange and completion, though some conveyancers now get this done before exchange as if it is not signed by the seller then completion cannot take place. The TR1 needs to be witnessed by an independent adult witness who should also sign the document.

****

Ch.6

Step-By-Step-Acting for the Purchaser

Purchasers Transaction Checklist-Checking initial purchaser Information

Existing client?

1. Full names and address of the clients
2. Estate agents details
3. Freehold or Leasehold
4. Price
5. Any preliminary deposit paid
6. Any fixtures and fittings being removed
7. Any instructions on completion date
8. Present or proposed use of the property
9. Who is resident at the property
10. How will any deposit be funded
11. How is the balance of the purchase price to be funded – that is has the client obtained a mortgage
12. Survey arrangements – is the property being surveyed?
13. Give advice of types of survey
14. How Is the property to be held – joint tenants or tenants in common

15. Check clients identity in accordance with the UK Finance Mortgage Lenders Handbook (see appendix 2).
16. Give notice of assignment of any lease if leasehold

Finances

Most purchasers proceed with a mortgage provided by a bank or a building society. There are also other sources of funds, such as Help-To-Buy funds and also funds from parents or friends, factored into the equation. Normally some sort of deposit is required, formerly ten-percent but now usually by negotiation. (not to be confused with the mortgage deposit). The purchaser and the solicitor would need to be satisfied that sufficient funds are available to complete the purchase before contracts are exchanged.

Mortgage considerations

The purchasers' solicitor is usually instructed by the lender to prepare the mortgage and obtain a good and marketable title for the lender. The lender secures his lending against the title by way of a legal mortgage. This is evidenced by the purchaser signing a mortgage deed and this being registered at the land registry as a charge.

The property cannot be sold without this charge being paid off. Lenders will normally only want and insist upon a first legal charge. This means they will have the right to enforce their charge by selling the property as mortgagee in possession in the event of the mortgage not being repaid.

In exchange for this the lender advances the money on the security of the property and the purchaser's solicitors' job is to make sure the funds are there at completion. The purchasers' solicitor will have to comply with all the conditions in the mortgage and submit a report on title. Once this has been accepted the funds will be available to complete.

The purchasers' solicitors will have to undertake an extra search on behalf of the lender which is a bankruptcy search confirming the purchaser is not bankrupt.

PURCHASERS IN FREEHOLD AND LEASEHOLD TRANSACTIONS-STEP BY STEP

1. Receiving Draft paperwork
2. Send copy plan to client
3. Checking
4. Check main points of contract with client i.e. price, names to go in the contract
5. Searches
6. Obtain fees from clients for searches (as outlined in chapter3) being:
7. Local search
8. Environmental search
9. Water search

10. Coal mining search if necessary
11. Commons registration search
12. When buying outside your area ask seller's solicitor's what are the usual searches?
13. Local land charge search – this will reveal
14. Planning permissions
15. Buildings regulation consent
16. If road adopted
17. Any road proposals
18. Any enforcement or planning notices
19. Environmental search
20. Coal search will reveal whether it is a coal mining area
21. Raising any preliminary enquiries
22. Official copy entries to the Title

You should check

- Description of the land according to the contract description
- Title number
- Estate – freehold or leasehold
- Easements
- Any rights of way
- Flying freeholds
- Proprietorship register
- Is the class of Title correct
- Is the seller the registered proprietor
- Any cautions or other entries on the Title
- Undertaking or release of the caution will be required

- Note any restrictive covenants referred to on the Title and advise the client, as this may affect their use and enjoyment of the premises. There may be covenants not to erect anything on the premises without the original owners consent
- Any missing covenants then consider an indemnity
- Any recent sales of the property as an under-value or no value.
- Consider insolvency of seller
- Contract/ Agreement
- Check the name of the seller is the same as the proprietorship register
- Similarly Title number
- Check special conditions
- Protocol Forms
- Fixtures fitting and contents – this is usually an extra to the contract to incorporate the chattels.
- Obtain client's approval of this prior to exchange of contracts
- Sellers Property Information Form (SPIF) check
- Boundaries
- Any guarantees
- Occupiers
- Any changes to the property for planning purposes
- Any disputes
- Leasehold sellers
- Leasehold information form

Leasehold enquiries - assignment of lease. The information required by the purchaser's solicitors is similar to a freehold transaction, with the additional details of the lease to be bought.

Items to be checked

- Landlord's consent required
- Length of the residue of term to be checked
- The lender may have specific requirements
- Check plan accurately identifies the property
- Any restrictions on sub-letting i.e. last 7 years
- Does the description of the property conform with the plan?
- Does the assignee have to enter into a direct covenant with the landlord. Are there covenants to enforce on behalf of the landlord
- Any covenants against the other tenants
- Check insurance complies with the lenders requirements
- Check service charge accounts for the last three years including receipt for the last sum payable.
- Request whether there is any potential change in the next year.
- Obtain receipt from last rent – similarly service charge
- Check whether any apportionment required
- Check whether any alterations to the premises, which would require landlords, consent.

Following all of the above steps undertaken by both the sellers and buyers solicitors it is now time to exchange contracts.

Ch.7

Reaching Exchange of Contracts

The Law Society's Formulae

Once the purchaser's and sellers have completed all the preliminary work and are ready to exchange, the buyer's solicitor indicates that the buyer is now ready to commit to a binding contract.

Obviously once contracts have been exchanged, neither party will be able to withdraw from the contract, and therefore all documents and arrangements will need to be checked thoroughly. If there is a dependant sale the solicitor must ensure that the exchange of contracts on both properties is synchronised to avoid leaving his client either owning two houses or being homeless.

If there is a failure of synchronisation it could be professional negligence.

Telephone

The main methods used for an exchange of contracts are: · Telephone exchange. · Personal exchange. · Postal exchange. · Document exchange. These are the most common methods of exchanging contracts. (Apart from a personal exchange no other method is entirely risk free). If contracts are exchanged at the telephone then the telephone conversation is the confirmation of exchange of contracts.

To avoid all uncertainties, the Law Society has agreed various formulae. The most important aspect of using any of the formulae is an accurate attendance note recording the telephone conversation must be made as soon as practicable.

A typical memorandum of exchange would include:

- Date
- Time
-
- Wording of any variations
- Identity of any parties to the conversation.
- Purchase price - agree Deposit

Any variation of the formulae, such as reduced deposit, must be expressly agreed and noted in writing.

Law Society Formula A

This is for use when one solicitor holds both signed parts of the Contract. The parties agree that exchange will take place from that moment and the solicitor holding both parts confirms that he or she undertakes by first class post or DX to send his or her signed part of the contract to the other solicitor, together with deposit as appropriate.

Law Society Formula B

For use where each solicitor holds his own client's signed part of the contract.

Each solicitor confirms to the other that he or she holds the signed part of the agreed form signed by the clients, and will forthwith insert the agreed completion date

Each solicitor undertakes to send by first class post or DX his or her signed part of the contract to the other together with the deposit if appropriate.

Law Society Formula C

Part 1

Each solicitor confirms that he or she holds the part of the contract in agreed form signed by his or her client,

Each solicitor undertakes to the other that, they will hold that part of the contract until part 2 of the formula takes place.

Part 2

Each solicitor undertakes to hold part of the contract in his or her possession to the other's order, so that contracts are exchanged at that moment and to send it to the other on that day.

This is effectively the giving and receiving of a release, which is as important as exchanging contracts.
The parties have to comply with the release within the agreed time frame.

When synchronising you normally arrange to receive a release on your sales transaction from your buyer's solicitor, with a time up to which it is effective.

When you have received your release on your sale you then give a release on your related purchase, with a slightly shorter time frame to allow you to exchange on the original transaction.

When your seller exchanges with you within the time that you have given to release, you then go to your purchaser and exchange within the time on the release given to you.

It is obviously essential to make sure that once you have exchanged on your sale that you immediately exchange on purchase. It is very important to have the terms of the release noted as carefully as if you were exchanging contracts, because one more phone call will then create an exchange of contract.

Client Care-Solicitors' Costs. Information and Client Care Code

The Client must be given cost information which must not be inaccurate or misleading, clearly in a way and a level which is appropriate to that particular client.

It should be confirmed in writing to the client as soon as possible. The basis of the firm's charges should be explained.

The solicitor should keep the client properly informed about costs as the matter progresses. The solicitor should tell the client, how much the costs are at regular intervals, like at least every six months and in appropriate cases delivering handbills at agreed intervals.

Complaints handling

The client must be told the name of the person in the firm to contact about any problems with the service provided. The firm must have a written complaints procedure to ensure that the complaints are handled in accordance with it and ensure the client is given a copy of the complaints procedure on request.

Stamp Duty Land Tax

Buyers Solicitor

Prior to completion the purchasers solicitor must obtain a stamp duty land tax form signed by the purchaser stating what, if any, stamp duty land tax should be paid. This must be submitted to HMRC whether duty is payable or not.

Stamp duty rates-Residential property rates

You usually pay Stamp Duty Land Tax (SDLT) on increasing portions of the property price above £500,000 (2020/2021) when you buy residential property, eg a house or flat. There are different rules if you're buying your first home and the purchase price is £500,000 or less. The rates below are for 2020/2021. Further details can be obtained from www.gov.uk/stamp-duty-land-tax.

You must still send an SDLT return for transactions under £500,000 unless they're exempt.

Rates from 8 July 2020 to 31 March 2021

You can also use this table to work out the SDLT for the purchase price of a lease (the 'lease premium').

Property or lease premium or transfer value	SDLT rate
Up to £500,000	ZERO
the next £425,000 (The portion from £500,001 to £925,000	5%
The next £575,000 (Te portion from £925,001 to £1.5million)	10%
The remaining amount (The portion above £1.5million)	12%

Example In March 2021 you buy a house for £625,000. The SDLT you owe will be calculated as follows:

- 0% on the first £500,000 = £0
- 5% on the remaining £125,000 = £6,250

total SDLT = £6,250

Rates from 1 April 2021

These rates also apply if you bought a property before 8 July 2020. You can also use this table to work out the SDLT for the purchase price of a lease (the 'lease premium').

Property or lease premium or transfer value	SDLT Rate
Up to £125,000	Zero
The next £125,000 (The portion from £125,001 to £250,000	2%
The next £675,000 (The portion from £250,001 to £925,000)	5%
The next £575,000 (The portion from £925,001 to £1.5 Million)	10%
The remaining amount (The portion above £1.5 million)	12%

Example In May 2021 you buy a house for £275,000. The SDLT you owe will be calculated as follows:

- 0% on the first £125,000 = £0
- 2% on the next £125,000 = £2,500
- 5% on the final £25,000 = £1,250

total SDLT = £3,750

If you're buying your first home

You can claim a discount (relief) if you buy your first home before 8 July 2020 or from 1 April 2021. This means you'll pay:

- no SDLT up to £300,000
- 5% SDLT on the portion from £300,001 to £500,000

You're eligible if you and anyone else you're buying with are first-time buyers. If the price is over £500,000, you follow the rules for people who've bought a home before.

New leasehold sales and transfers

When you buy a new residential leasehold property you pay SDLT on the purchase price of the lease (the 'lease premium') using the rates above.

If the total rent over the life of the lease (known as the 'net present value') is more than the SDLT threshold), you'll pay SDLT at 1% on the portion of net present value over:

- £500,000 for purchases from 8 July 2020 to 31 March 2021
- £125,000 for purchases from 1 April 2021
- This does not apply to existing ('assigned') leases.

Higher rates for additional properties

You'll usually have to pay 3% on top of SDLT rates if buying a new residential property means you'll own more than one. You may not have to pay the higher rates if you exchanged contracts before 26 November 2015.

If you're replacing your main residence

You will not pay the extra 3% SDLT if the property you're buying is replacing your main residence and that has already been sold. If you have not sold your main residence on the day you complete your new purchase you'll have to pay higher rates. This is because you own 2 properties.

You can apply for a refund if you sell your previous main home within 36 months. There are special rules if you own property with someone else or already own a property outside England, Wales and Northern Ireland.

If it takes longer than 36 months to sell your previous main home

You may still be able to get a refund of the extra 3% SDLT if:

- you purchased your new home on or after 1 January 2017
- the delay was outside your control, for example because of coronavirus (COVID-19) or a public authority blocking the sale
- you have now sold your old home

To claim a refund, write to HMRC and explain why the sale took longer than 36 months. Include:

- your details
- details of the main buyer - if different to your own

- details of the property where higher rate SDLT was paid - including the address, date of purchase and SDLT unique transaction reference number
- details of the previous main residence - including the address, date of sale and SDLT unique transaction reference number
- the amount of higher rate SDLT paid
- the amount of tax you're asking for a repayment of
- a bank account and sort code for the person receiving the payment

Special rates

There are different SDLT rules and rate calculations for:

- corporate bodies
- people buying 6 or more residential properties in one transaction
- Shared ownership properties
- multiple purchases or transfers between the same buyer and seller ('linked purchases')
- purchases that mean you own more than one property
- Companies and Trusts buying residential property

****

Ch. 8

Completion and Post-Completion

Between exchange of contracts and completion –Preparing for Completion-Sellers checklist

- Check Transfer has been approved and requisitions replied to
- Received engrossed transfer from buyer – sign plan of the transfer.
- Seller to execute transfer in time for completion.
- Obtain mortgage redemption figure from mortgagees relating to all mortgages

Discharge of sellers' Mortgage.

Most sellers have mortgages and this will need to be cleared on completion. The seller's solicitors will obtain the redemption figure that is the figure to clear the mortgage on completion.

Once this has been ascertained it is usually paid off on completion by bank transfer. The seller's solicitors give an undertaking to do this and provide in due course either an END being a electronic notification of discharge or DS1 which is a paper discharge that needs to be lodged with the purchase document at the land registry. Follow the steps below:

- For leasehold obtain last receipts and make any apportionment necessary
- Prepare completion statement where necessary and send copies to buyer's solicitor in time for completion.
- Prepare an undertaking that needs to be given on completion for discharge of mortgage
- Locate title deeds and schedule to be handed over on completion
- Check arrangements for vacant possession and handing over keys
- Ensure estate agents are aware of completion arrangements
- Prepare bill and send to client

Documents to be handed over on completion

- Title deeds if unregistered, no land or charge certificate since October 2003, due to de-materialisation of deeds.
- END/ DS1 or undertaking
- Any money received for fixtures and fittings
- Arrange for keys to be released by agents

Between exchange of contracts and completion –Preparing for Completion-buyers checklist

1. Transfer approved and requisitions satisfactorily answered
2. Give power to execute mortgage deed, purchase deed and plan

3. Send executed transfer (TR1) to sellers solicitors in sufficient time for his client to sign prior to completion. Although as mentioned this can be signed before exchange of contracts, in readiness.
4. Do pre-completion searches – such as bankruptcy, OS1 for purchaser whole, OS2, purchaser part. carry out a Company search
5. Make report on title to lender and request advance cheque in time for completion
6. Received completion statement where necessary
7. Remind client of arrangements for completion
8. Check property insured
9. Check arrangements for vacant possession and handing over of keys
10. Ensure estate agents are aware on completion arrangements
11. Make arrangements for transmission of completion money to sellers solicitors on the day of completion or where he has directed

AFTER COMPLETION – SELLERS CHECKLIST

1. Confirm receipt of funds
2. Telephone buyer's solicitors
3. Telephone estate agent to confirm completion and authorise release of keys
4. Inform client that completion has taken place

5. Send Title Deeds and other relevant documents by first class post. DX on date of completion
6. Transfer any purchase funds on related purchase
7. Discharge existing mortgage by CHAPS or cheque with END or DS1 as required
8. Pay estate agent's commission account
9. Account to client for balance of proceeds of sale
10. Transfer costs if agreed
11. On receipt of DS1 or confirmation of END send or inform purchaser's solicitors and ask to be released from undertaking previously given to them.
12. Remind client to cancel buildings insurance and notify public utilities
13. Remind client of any Capital Gains Tax assessment which may be due
14. Check file before placing in dead system

AFTER COMPLETION – BUYERS CHECKLIST

1. Inform Client and Lender that completion has taken place
2. Complete Mortgage Deed
3. Complete file copies of Mortgage Deed and other relevant documents

Arrange payment of Stamp Duty on the SDLT form. As this form now has to be signed by the purchaser's it would be wise to have this signed prior to completion at the same time as the transfer.

If acting for a Company, register charge at Company's House within 21 days. This time limit is absolute and cannot be extended without an order of the court. Failing to register within the time limit will be an act of negligence by the solicitor.

Pay off and deal with any undertakings concerning finance. Once SDLT form clear by the Revenue, and you are in receipt of the DS1 or END, register at Land Registry.On receipt of DS1 or confirmation of END, release seller's solicitors from their undertaking.

Make application to the Land registry for Registration of Title within the relevant priority period.

Serve a notice of assignment of Life policies or lease.

On receipt of Title Information document from the Land Registry, check contents carefully.

Deal with the custody of Deeds in accordance with the client's instructions or send to Lender to be held by them during the continuance of the Mortgage.

****

Glossary

A

Acting for both parties -There are limited circumstances when solicitors can act for both parties

Amount outstanding on the mortgage-Also known as the redemption figure

Apportionment of the purchase price-This may be used to save stamp duty land tax. Fixtures and fittings known as chattels do not attract stamp duty and this is why the distinction between those and land is important.

Attorneys-A deed may be signed by an attorney but evidence of his power of attorney must be produced as this will be required by the land registry.

Auctions-The auction contract is usually prepared in advance. The purchaser has the right to undertake all his searches and enquiries and survey before the auction.

Once the auction has been concluded usually a ten per cent deposit is taken and the sale takes place 28 days later. It would be necessary for anyone entering into an auction to have their finance in place before the hammer falls.

B

Boundaries-Even with a registered title the boundaries shown on the filed plan are general boundaries and are not definitive. The rule is generally what has been there for the last 12 years is the boundary this may have to be supported by statutory declarations.

Breach of a Restrictive Covenant-Or other defect. Indemnity insurance might be available

Bridging Finance -This might be for a deposit which is repaid on the sale of the property. It is rare for English banks to extend finance for a property that is open ended. It is usually only extended once contracts are exchange and there is a fixed date for completion.

Building Regulation Consent-This may be required even if there are not developments that require planning permission. It relates to health and safety matters and the type of materials used on completion of building works for which consent it required a final certificate must be obtained from the local authority. This is evidence that the building regulations have been complied with.

C

Capital Gains Tax-The main exemption which affects residential conveyancing is the principal private dwelling house exemption

The seller must have occupied the dwelling house as his only or main residence throughout the period of ownership There is a sliding scale for absences and exemptions of short periods of absence

Capacity-The seller might be sole owner, joint owner, personal representative mortgagee, charity, company bankrupt or otherwise incapacitated.

Classes of Title-There are different classes of title the best being absolute title but there is also possessory title qualified title and good leasehold title

Contaminated Land -Any contamination could have serious effects in that it may be impossible to sell or obtain a mortgage on.

Completion-The day on which the transaction is finalised, the money changes hands and the parties vacate and take possession of the land that is the moving day.

Co-Ownership-This is where more than one person owns the land such as tenant in common or joint tenant.

Conveyancing-The process of transferring the ownership of freehold and leasehold land.

Compulsory Registration-This has arisen since 1990 and applies to the whole of England and Wales. The categories of events triggering a registration have changed but it is still not compulsory to register land without one of these triggers but voluntary registration could take place.

Conservation Area-Any non listed building in a conservation area must not be demolished with conservation area consent. There are also restrictions on development.

Contract Races -This is where more than one contract has been issued solicitors are obliged to let both parties know the terms of the race that is what needs to be done to secure the property. It must be confirmed in writing. A standard contact race would specific that the first person to be in a position to exchange contracts unconditionally wins the race. This is usually signified by the purchasers solicitors producing a signed contract and deposit cheque together with authority to proceed.

Covenants-This is a promise made in a deed and binding any subsequent owner of the land they may include such matter as maintaining the fences and only using the land for the erection of one property.

D

Deeds-Apart from unregistered land most deeds have now dematerialised as they are registered at the land registry.

Evidence of ownership is shown by official copies of the registered entries. This is an official dated document showing the current state of the title.

Deposit-Although not a legal requirement is it customary and it's a form of security and part payment towards the purchase price.

Discharge of seller's mortgage-On completion is the seller has a mortgage this will need to be paid off and evidence given to the purchasers solicitor. This will need to be lodged at the land registry as proof of the discharge before a new purchaser can be substituted and maybe a new mortgage started.

Draft contract-The name attached to the contract before it is agreed by the parties and prior to exchange of contracts. Once the contract is approved it can be signed by the parties and forms the basis of the transactions. They must be in the same format. Identical contracts are exchanged.

E

Easements-This is a right over land of another such as a right of way or of light.

Engrossment-Merely means properly typed up version of a document the draft is amended then the engrossment is the fair copy

Escrow-A document such as contract mortgage transfer is delivered and will not become effective until some future date. It is therefore held in escrow the condition being that the event takes place such as completion or exchange of contracts. Gets rid of the need for all the parties to a transaction being in the same room at the same time.

Exchange of contracts-When the parties agree to bind themselves legally to buy and sell the land.

Execution-Means the signing of a document in a certain way for a deed to be valid it must contain the words this deed signed by the necessary parties in the presence of a witness and be delivered.

F

Filed plan-In conveyancing a plan is a map showing the land referred to edged in red. It is the official designation of the land for land registry purposes

Fixture and fittings-Now a formal part of the process in that purchasers solicitor will expect to see a completed fixtures and fittings form. It may be acceptable to apportion part of the price for fixtures and fittings and this is sometimes undertaken when the price falls on one of the bands for change in stamp duty. The list must be legitimate ad the revenue have the right to query this and levy any tax not paid

Fixtures and fittings distinction-Between objects not attached to the land are fittings and those attached are fixtures. The current fixtures and fitting list covers most eventualities but care should be taken if an offer is deemed to include items at the property they should be specifically mentioned in the contract.

Full Survey-As the name suggests this is full survey of the property and should contain a detailed breakdown of every aspect of the property.

H

Home Buyers Valuation and Survey Report-This is a compromise between a full structural survey and valuation.

I

Insurance-The risk on the property passes when contracts are exchanged. Even thought he purchaser has not got possession. The property is usually also insured by the seller up until the date of completion. They both have an insurable risk.

Indemnity Covenants-Any owner of land will remain liable for the covenants and passes these on by way of an indemnity covenant by any incoming purchaser

Investigating Title-Once the seller has produced the contract package the purchasers solicitors investigate title. This is to ensure that the seller is the owner of the property which is the subject of the contract. Also it must not reveal any defects other than those can be rectified prior to exchange of contracts. There may for instance be consent required from a third party such as the necessity to register the transfer of a lease and become the member of a management company.

J

Joint tenants-This is most common between husband and wife. Both own equal shares in the property if either were to die the other inherit by way of survivorship. They cannot leave their share by will to anyone else.

L

Listed Building-Where a building might be of outstanding historic or architectural important the secretary of state may list it. Any alterations to the property will require both planning permission and listed building consent.

M

Mortgage-Is where the owner of land borrows money on the security of the land Also known as a legal charge. The lender has certain statutory powers the most important being that they can sell the property in the event of the loan not being paid.

Mortgage Fraud-Normally some proof of identity is required but this has been overtaken by the money laundering rules whereby it is accepted practice that clients should produce to their solicitors all the usual forms of ID to include utility bills driving licence passport etc.

Mortgages Repayments-The main types of repayment are pension, endowment and interest only. They do not affect the conveyancing transaction but some may have slightly different procedures between the conveyancers and the lender such as notices or deposit of insurance policies.

O

Occupiers Rights-The most important is the spouse of the seller. They have a statutory right to occupy the matrimonial home. Usually an enquiry is made as to there being any other occupiers of the matrimonial home. They are then asked to sign the contract to confirm they will give vacant possession completion.

Office Copy Entries-Usually refers to the registered title but can relate to any official copy issued by the land or other registries. They are acceptable as the originals.

Overriding Interests-These are matters affecting the land which are not on the register although this is being resolved under the current land registry rules. The most important being rights of way not mentioned on the deeds local land charges squatters rights.

P

Planning - Use of the property-It should be checked that the property has permission for its current use. Any purchaser should be aware that any change of use form its current use may require planning permission. For example a residential property may not be used for the fixing and selling of cars without a change of use. Any breach will be enforced by the local planning authority.

Planning Breach-This could be rectified by retrospective permission or again by indemnity insurance.

Purchase Deed-Now the transfer or TR1 this is the document that is signed by the seller transferring the land from the seller to the purchaser. It is signed prior to completion and once the formalities have been finalised such as the passing of the money it will be forwarded to the purchasers solicitors. This document will need to be stamped and registered at the land registry.

Possessory Title-The registry may grant a possessory title in the event of lack of paper title and eventually it can be upgraded to an absolute title. Land can be acquired through adverse possession but it is still subject to all covenants and easements etc existing at the date of the registration

Post Contract Stage-Between exchange of contracts and completion essential things such as finance is resolved as our final searches and all documents signed in readiness for completion.

R

Radon-If the property is in an area affected by radon gas a specific search should be undertaken which will reveal whether a survey has been undertaken and remedial measures have been taken.

Registered land-A state run system that proves the ownership of land by have a title registered at the HM land registry.

S

Searches-There are a series of searches. Before exchange of contracts the local authority search, after exchange bankruptcy and land registry searches.

Special Conditions-Any special condition will be used to vary the standard conditions of sale contained in the contract

Subject to Contract-This is of historical interest now as it is not possible to exchange contracts inadvertently or entering into irrevocably buying land without a proper contract. Some organisations still insist on using it as it gives them comfort Not now necessary in view of the Law Of Property (Miscellaneous) Provisions act 1989

Survey-There are many kinds of survey form the mere valuation by a lender to a full structural survey. Any purchaser should be aware that at the moment the law says *caveat emptor* that is let the buyer beware. Apart form a deliberate misstatement the seller is not liable for the current state of the property. An invariable practice is for purchasers to be advised to have a survey of the property and not to rely solely on the building society valuation.

Title-Either the registered or unregistered proof of the seller's ownership of the land.

Title Number-Every piece of registered land has a unique title number and must be used in all official documents searches etc.
Tenants in Common-Is where two or more people own land jointly in separate shares. Either owner can pass their share by will to anyone they wish.

Tenure-The legal term for how the land is being held being either freehold or leasehold.

U

Unregistered Land-The seller has to prove title by a series of documents such as conveyances, mortgagees etc now being replaced by registered conveyancing.

Undertakings-These are promises by solicitor to undertake certain acts. The most common being that the sellers solicitor will discharge the existing mortgage. Failure to comply with the undertaking is a professional offence so therefore they will not be entered into lightly and can be relied up They should always be confirmed in writing and their terms made certain.

Upgrading Title-Either on application or on the initiative of the registrar a title may be upgraded such as possessory to absolute and the same for qualified and good leasehold title

V

Valuation-Can either be an estate agents valuation which is a financial matter for the purchasers and sellers a lenders valuation is the figure that is used to calculate how much the lender is prepared to lend. This is based on a valuers report prepared for the lender once the buyer has requested a loan. It is an assessment of the value not a survey of the property. Lenders will normally exclude liability for any defects in the property. They are not undertaking that the property is fit for its purpose just because they are prepared to lend on it.

Value Added Tax – VAT-Is payable on solicitors costs but not o the purchase price of second hand properties. There is not VAT payable on stamp duty or land registry fees in a domestic transaction.

Recommended Reading

Law Society Conveyancing Protocol, 2019 Obtainable from the Law Society Bookshop.

https://www.lawsociety.org.uk/topics/property/conveyancing-protocol

****

Appendix 1

SALE AND PURCHASE OF PROPERTY

STANDARD LETTERS

Letter to Building Society / Bank Requesting Title Deeds

9 November, 2020

Address

Dear Sirs

Re Property:

Account Number:

Borrower:

We act for the above named clients in connection with the sale of the above property and we shall be obliged if you would please send us have the Title Deeds relating to this property.

We undertake to hold them to your order pending redemption of the mortgage.

At the same time please let us know the amount owing under this mortgage.

Yours faithfully

Letter to Estate Agent Acknowledging Sales Particulars

9 November, 2020

Address

Dear Sirs

Re Property:

Our Client:

We acknowledge safe receipt of your sales particulars and we confirm we have today contacted the purchaser's solicitors with a view to issuing a draft Contract.

Yours faithfully

Authority to Bank to Obtain Title Deeds

9 November, 2020

Address

Dear Sirs

We hereby give you authority to release the Title Deeds for property listed below to ……………. of …………….

Address of Property: ……………………………………

Address of Lender: ……………………………………

Account Number: ……………………………………

Signature ……………………………………

Signature ……………………………………

First Letter to Purchaser's Solicitors

9 November, 2020

Address

Dear Sirs

Re Property:

Your Client:

Our Client:

We understand that you act on behalf of ??????? of ????????????? in connection with their proposed purchase of the above from our clients ??????????????.

We would be obliged if you could confirm that if your clients have a property to sell a purchaser has been found and if your client should require finance this has been approved at least in principle.

Subject to the above being confirmed we will arrange for a draft Contract to be issued to you as soon as possible.

Yours faithfully

Letter Issuing Contract etc to Purchaser's Solicitors

9 November, 2020

Address

Dear Sirs

Re Property:

Your Client:

Our Client:

Thank you for your letter of ????????. We take this opportunity of enclosing:

Draft Contract in duplicate

Official Copy of Register Entries plus File Plan

Fixtures Fittings and Contents List

Seller's Property Information Form

Copy Transfer dated ???????????

Yours faithfully

Letter to Purchaser' Solicitor on Completion

9 November, 2020

Address

Dear Sirs

Re Property:

Your Client:

Our Client:

We acknowledge safe receipt of your Telegraphic Transfer in the sum of £........ and we take this opportunity of enclosing the following:

TR1

Land Certificate number ....

All Pre-registration documents

Kindly acknowledge safe receipt.

We confirm that we have today telephoned the agents to release the keys.

Yours faithfully

Letter Sending Approved TR1 and Replies to Requisitions on Title

9 November, 2020

Address

Dear Sirs

Re Property:

Your Client:

Our Client:

Thank you for your letter of ………… we take this opportunity of enclosing the following:

TR1 approved as amended

Requisitions on Title and our replies thereto

Yours faithfully

Letter to Purchaser's Solicitor on Exchange of Contracts

9 November, 2020

Address

Dear Sirs

Re Property:

Your Client:

Our Client:

Further to our telephone conversation at 2:15 p.m. between ...... and .... Contracts were exchanged and the date fixed for completion is ....

The sale price is £....... and you will be holding the £........ deposit strictly to our order pending completion.

We enclose our client's part of the Contract to complete exchange of Contracts. .

Yours faithfully

Letter to Estate Agents requesting Commission Account

9 November, 2020

Address

Dear Sirs

Re Property:

Client:

We write to confirm Contracts have now been exchanged in this matter. The date fixed for completion being the ……….

We await hearing from you with your commission account.

Yours faithfully

Letter to Bank/Building Society Requesting Redemption Figure

9 November, 2020

Building Society
Address

Dear Sirs

Re: Borrower:

Property:

Account No:

Would you please let us have the redemption figure on the above mortgage account as at *date*.......

Yours faithfully

Letter Informing Utilities of Sale

9 November, 2020

Address

Dear Sirs

Re Owner:

Property:

Account No:

We take this opportunity of advising you that the above property has now been sold and as from ………………… the new occupants will be ……………….

Yours faithfully

PURCHASE PROPERTY

STANDARD LETTERS

First Letter to Seller's Solicitors

9 November, 2020

Address

For the attention of:

Dear Sirs

Re Property:

Our Client:

Your Client:

We act on behalf of .... and .... our clients finance is approved in principle and we await hearing from you with draft paperwork.

Yours faithfully

Letter to Seller's Solicitor Returning Draft Contract Approved

9 November, 2020

Address

For the attention of:

Dear Sirs

Re Property:

Our Client:

Your Client:

Thank you for your letter of .... we take this opportunity of enclosing the draft Contract duly approved.

We will use the top copy as the engrossment.

Yours faithfully

Letter to Seller's Solicitor on Exchange of Contracts

9 November, 2020

Address

Dear Sirs

Re Property:

Your Client:

Our Client:

Further to our telephone conversation at 2:15 p.m. between …… and ……… …… Contracts were exchanged and the date fixed for completion is …………..

The purchase price is £……. and we will be holding the £…….. deposit strictly to your order pending completion.

We enclose our client's part of the Contract to complete exchange of Contracts. .

Yours faithfully

Letter to Seller's Solicitors Sending TR1 with Requisitions on Title

9 November, 2020

Address

Dear Sirs

Re Property:

Your Client:

Our Client:

Thank you for your letter of ………… we take this opportunity of enclosing the following:

TR1 in duplicate

Requisitions on Title

Yours faithfully

Letter to Seller's Solicitor Confirming Purchase Money Sent

9 November, 2020

Address

Dear Sirs

Re Property:

Your Client:

Our Client:

We are writing to confirm we have today telegraphically transferred to you the sum of £……….. being the balance required to complete this matter.

We await hearing from you with a dated and executed Transfer and all the other Title Deeds relating to the property.

We would be obliged if on receipt of the money you could kindly telephone the agents to release the keys.

Yours faithfully

Appendix 2

Overview of the UK Finance Lenders' Handbook for conveyancers in England and Wales (Formerly the Council of Mortgage Lenders Handbook.

The lender's handbook provides comprehensive instructions for conveyancers acting on behalf of lenders in residential conveyancing transactions. It is divided into two parts:
Part 1 sets out the main instructions
Part 2 details each lenders specific requirements relating to the main instructions.
There is a chance of a conflict of interest if you are acting for both the borrower and the lender. If there is any conflict of interest you should refuse to act for one or other of the parties.
You can only reveal information to the lender if the borrower agrees, if the borrower refuses to agree you must return mortgage instructions to the lender.

Communications

All communications with the lender must be in writing, quoting the mortgage account or roll number and the clients name etc.

Safeguards

A proof of identity of borrowers
You must follow the guidance of the Law Society's Money Laundering Regulations 2017
Proof of identity can be one from List A and one from List B

Identity - List A

Current signed passport

Valid UK driving licence

EEA member state identity card

Address-List B

UK/EU/EEA Drivers Licence (if UK Drivers Licence not used as ID)

Must be valid, not expired. Photo only. Full or provisional.

Bank, Building Society or Credit Union Statement

Dated with 3 months. Must include account number and show recent activity. No general correspondence.

Credit Card Statement

Dated within 3 months. Must include account number and show recent activity. No general correspondence.

UK, EU, EEA Mortgage statement

Dated within 12 months. Must show account number. No general correspondence.

Utility Bill

Dated within 6 months E.g. Gas, electricity, water. Must show address for service and/or account number. No general correspondence.

Telephone Bill

Dated within 6 months E.g. Landline or mobile pay monthly (excluding pay as you go). Must show address for service and/or account number. No general correspondence.

Council Tax

Dated within 12 months. Must show address for service and/or account number. No general correspondence.

Tenancy Agreement

Dated with 12 months. Must state full name and full property address. Issued by local council, housing association, solicitor or reputable letting agent.

Benefits Entitlement Letter

Dated within 12 months. Issued by DWP or Jobcentre plus. Must confirm benefit payable at time of issue. E.g. Pension, disability, single parent, housing etc.

HMRC Tax Notification

Dated with 6 months. Must state national insurance number and tax calculation. No general correspondence.

Home or Motor Insurance Certificate

Dated within 12 months. Must state insured address or registered address for vehicle and policy number. No general correspondence.

UK solicitors letter confirming house purchase/land registration

Dated with 3 months. Must state full name of new proprietor and full property address.

NHS Medical Card or letter from GP confirming registration

Dated within 3 months. Must state individual's date of birth and NHS number. No general correspondence.

Official confirmation of Electoral Register entry or official poll card

Dated within 12 months. Must state full name and full address. No general correspondence.

Police Registration Certificate

Dated within 12 months. Must state the full residential address of the individual.

In addition, to satisfy the regulations:

Probate

If person is acting as a Representative of an Estate you should require the following:

Grant of Probate (if a will was left)

Letter of administration (if no will left)

Individual identity evidence from List A & B for the Personal Representative, either executor or administrator

Limited company

If a person is acting as a Representative of a UK Company you will also require the following:

Certificate of Incorporation

Articles of Association

Memorandum of Association

Latest Annual Return or Confirmation Statement, with details of current company officers

If offshore, nominee director declaration and a general power of attorney

Individual identity evidence from List A and B for all individuals or entities with 25% or more of the shares or voting rights in the company

If a person is acting as a Representative of an Offshore Company you will also require the following:

Certificate of Incorporation

Articles of Association, Memorandum of Association, Latest Annual Return with details of current company officers, Share Certificate(s) showing the Ultimate Beneficial Owner OR

Certificate of Incumbency

If the shares are owned by another company, repeat steps above for the holding company.

Nominee director declaration and/or general Power of Attorney (if applicable)

Individual identity evidence from List A and B for all individuals or entities with 25% or more of the shares or voting rights in the company

Trust

If a person is acting as a Representative of a Trust you require the following:

Trust deed

List of trustees

List of beneficiaries

Individual Identity evidence from List A & B for all individuals with a vest interest in 25% or more of the capital and/or those who exercise control over the Trust

Valuation of the property.

The borrower should be advised not to rely upon the report

Re-inspection

Where a final inspection is needed you must ask for the final inspection at least 10 working days before the advance is required.

Title and surrounding circumstances

If the owner or registered proprietor has been registered for less than six months, or if the seller is not the registered proprietor this must be reported unless - the person represented is the registered proprietor of an institution or mortgagee exercising power of sales are receiving bankruptcy, liquidator or developer or builder, selling the property under part exchange scheme.

Searches and reports

You must make all the usual necessary searches and enquiries.

A lender should be named as the applicant in the HM Land Registry search.

All searches except where there is a priority, period must be no more than six months old at completion

All of the searches such as mining searches should be undertaken in the areas affected and for personal searches and search insurance, they should be checked in part two.

Planning and Building Regulations

The property must have the benefit of any necessary planning consent

Having a good and marketable title

The title of the property must be good and marketable, free of any restrictions, covenants, easement, charges or encumbrances, which might reasonably be expected to adversely affect the value of the property.

Flying Freeholds

Freehold flats and other freehold arrangements. Each individual lender will have its own requirements.

Restrictions on use and occupation

Any material restrictions on its use should be reported, such as occupier's employment, age or income.

Restrictive Covenants

You must enquire whether the property is being built, altered or is currently used in breach in of a restrictive covenant.

First Legal Charge

They require a fully enforceable first charge by way of legal mortgage over the property. All existing charges must be redeemed on or before completion.

Leasehold Property

A period of an unexpired lease as set out in part two. There must be no provision for forfeiture on insolvency of the tenant or any superior tenant. There must be satisfactory legal rights for access services, support, shelter and protection.

There must be adequate covenants in respect of building insurance, maintenance, repair of structure, foundations, main walls, roof etc.

You should ensure that responsibility of the insurance, maintenance and repair of the services is through the common services that of the landlord or one or more of the tenants of the building that forms one or more of a management company.

The lease must contain adequate provisions for the enforcement of these obligations of the landlord or Management Company.
If the terms of the lease are unsatisfactory, you must obtain a suitable deed of variation, or indemnity insurance: see part two.
You must obtain on completion the clear receipt or written confirmation of the last payment of ground rent and service charge from the landlord or the managing agent.

Notice of the mortgage must be served on the landlord or any management company.

It must be reported if the landlord is either absent or insolvent

A recent article in the Law Society Gazette stated that a frequent ground for complaint arises when insufficient checks are made by buyer's solicitors to ensure that ground rent, service charges and other outgoings relating to leasehold purchases are paid up to date on completion.

It is both prudent and good practice for the buyer's solicitors to contact the managing agents for the properties directly or to ensure that the seller's solicitors do so.

Solicitors will then be able to ensure that the documentary evidence is available in relation to the payment of ground rents and service charges including apportionment's where appropriate. They can also confirm whether the freehold holder or superior landlord is planning any future improvement or remedial work and can consider the benefit if negotiating a retention with landlord's solicitors to protect their client's. A solicitors omission to seek and to clarify information available from managing agents may result in inadequate professional service.

Management company

The Management Company must have the legal right to enter the property. You should make a company search and prove that the company is in existence and registered at Company's House. You should obtain the management companies last three years published accounts.

INSOLVENCY CONSIDERATIONS

You must obtain a clear Bankruptcy search against the borrower. You must certify that any entries do not relate to the borrower. If the property is subject to deed of gift or transaction at an apparent undervalue, completed in under five years of the proposed mortgage you must be satisfied that the lender will be protected, if not arrange indemnity insurance.

You must obtain a clear bankruptcy search against all parties between a deed of gift or transaction that is an apparent under value.

POWERS OF ATTORNEY

Any document that is being executed under a Power of Attorney, you must ensure that the Power of Attorney is properly drawn, appears to be properly executed and the Attorney knows of no reason why such Power of Attorney will not be subsisting at completion.

Power of Attorney must not be used in connection with a regulated loan under the Consumer Credit Act 1974. The original certified copy of the Power of Attorney must be sent with the deeds.

THE PROPERTY

Boundaries

These must be clearly defined by reference to a suitable plan or description.

Purchase price

This must be the same as set out in the instructions. Must advise the lender if there are any cash back or non-cash incentives.

Vacant possession

It is the term of the loan that Vacant possession is obtained unless otherwise stated.

New Properties

You must ensure that there is a National House Building Council Buildmark Scheme or similar.

Roads and Sewers

If not adopted, there must be a suitable agreement or a bond in existence.

Easements

All reasonable steps to check the property has the benefit of all easements.

Insurance

Where the lender does not arrange any insurance this must be arranged so that cover starts no later than completion.

Other occupiers

Rights of interested persons who are not a party to the mortgage who are or who will be in occupation of the premises may affect their right and you must obtain a signed deed or form of consent from all occupants age 17 or over.

Signing and Witnessing of Documents

Witnessing of documents is considered good practice so that the signature of a document that needs to be witnessed is witnessed by a solicitor, legal executive or licensed conveyancer.

All documents required at completion must be dated with the date of completion of the loan. After completion you must register the mortgage with the HM Land Registry.

Your mortgage file.

For evidential purposes you must keep your file for at least six years from the date of the mortgage before destroying it.

Legal Costs

All charges and disbursements are payable by the buyer and should be collected on or before completion. Non payment of fees or disbursements should not delay the stamping and registration of documents.

****

Appendix 3

Example of some of the main Protocol Forms to be used in conveyancing

PROTOCOL FORMS (see overleaf)

Form 1 TA6 Law Society property information Form (3rd Edition)
Form 2.TA7 Leasehold Information Form (2nd Ed)
Form 3, TA10 Law Society Fitting and Contents form
Form 4. TR1 Transfer of Whole

****

Property Information Form

Address of the property

Full names of the seller

Seller's conveyancer

Name of firm

Address

Email

Reference

This form is completed by the seller to supply detailed information and documents which may be relied upon for the conveyancing process. It is important that sellers and buyers read the notes below.

Definitions

"Seller" means all sellers together if the property is owned by more than one person

"Buyer" means all buyers together if the property is being bought by more than one person.

"Property" includes all the buildings and land within the boundaries

Instructions to the Seller

- Answers should be prepared by the person or persons who are named as owner on the deeds or Land Registry title or by the owner's legal representative(s) if selling under a power of attorney or grant of representation. If there is more than one seller, you should prepare the answers together or, if only one seller prepares the form, the other(s) should check the answers given and all sellers should sign the form.

- If you do not know the answer to any question, you must say so. If you are unsure of the meaning of any questions or answers, please ask your conveyancer. Completing this form is not mandatory, but omissions or delay in providing some information may delay the sale.

- If you later become aware of any information which would alter any replies you have given, you must inform your conveyancer immediately. This is as important as giving the right answers in the first place. Do not change any arrangements concerning the property with anyone (such as a tenant or a neighbour) without first consulting your conveyancer.

- It is very important that your answers are accurate. If you give incorrect or incomplete information to the buyer (on this form or otherwise in writing or in conversation, whether through your estate agent or conveyancer or directly to the buyer), the buyer may make a claim for compensation from you or refuse to complete the purchase.

- You should answer the questions based upon information known to you (or, in the case of legal representatives, you or the owner). You are not expected to have expert knowledge of legal or technical matters, or matters that occurred prior to your ownership of the property.

- Please give your conveyancer any letters, agreements or other papers which help answer the questions. If you are aware of any which you are not supplying with the answers, tell your conveyancer. If you do not have any documentation you may need to obtain copies at your own expense. Also pass to your conveyancer any notices you have received concerning the property and any which arrive at any time before completion of the sale.

Instructions to the buyer

- If the seller gives you, separately from this form, any information concerning the property (in writing or in conversation, whether through an estate agent or solicitor or directly to you) on which you wish to rely when buying the property, you should tell your conveyancer.

- You are entitled to rely on the replies given to enquiries but in relation to the physical condition of the property, the replies should not be treated as a substitute for undertaking your own survey or making your own independent enquiries, which you are recommended to do.

- The seller is only obliged to give answers based on their own information. They may not have knowledge of legal or technical matters. You should not expect the seller to have knowledge of, or give information about, matters prior to their ownership of the property.

1 Boundaries

1.1 Looking towards the property from the road, who owns or accepts responsibility to maintain or repair the boundary features:

(a) On the left? ☐ Seller ☐ Neighbour ☐ Shared ☐ Not known

(b) On the right? ☐ Seller ☐ Neighbour ☐ Shared ☐ Not known

(c) At the rear? ☐ Seller ☐ Neighbour ☐ Shared ☐ Not known

(d) At the front? ☐ Seller ☐ Neighbour ☐ Shared ☐ Not known

1.2 If the boundaries are irregular please indicate ownership by written description or by reference to a plan:

1.3 Is the seller aware of any boundary feature having been moved in the last 20 years? If Yes, please give details: ☐ Yes ☐ No

1.4 During the seller's ownership, has any land previously forming part of the property been sold or any adjacent property purchased? If Yes, please give details: ☐ Yes ☐ No

1.5 Does any part of the property or any building on the property overhang, or project under, the boundary of the neighbouring property or road? If Yes, please give details: ☐ Yes ☐ No

1.6 Has any notice been received under the Party Wall Act 1996 in respect of any shared/party boundaries? If Yes, please supply a copy, and give details of any works carried out or agreed: ☐ Yes ☐ No ☐ Enclosed ☐ To follow

2 Disputes and complaints

2.1 Have there been any disputes or complaints regarding this property or a property nearby? If Yes, please give details: ☐ Yes ☐ No

2.2 Is the seller aware of anything which might lead to a dispute about the property or a property nearby? If Yes, please give details: ☐ Yes ☐ No

3. Notices and proposals

3.1 Have any notices or correspondence been received or sent (e.g. from or to a neighbour, council or government department), or any negotiations or discussions taken place, which affect the property or a property nearby? If Yes, please give details: ☐ Yes ☐ No

3.2 Is the seller aware of any proposals to develop property or land nearby, or of any proposals to make alterations to buildings nearby? If Yes, please give details: ☐ Yes ☐ No

4. Alterations, planning and building control

Note to seller: Please provide copies of all relevant approvals and supporting paperwork referred to in section 4 of this form, such as listed building consents, planning permissions, Building Regulations consents and completion certificates. If you have had works carried out you should produce the documentation authorising this. Copies may be obtained from the relevant local authority website. Competent Persons Certificates may be obtained from the contractor or the scheme provider (eg FENSA or Gas Safe Register). *For further information about Competent Persons Certificates go to: www.gov.uk.*

Note to buyer: If any alterations or improvements have been made since the property was last valued for council tax, the sale of the property may trigger a revaluation. This may mean that following completion of the sale, the property will be put into a higher council tax band. *For further information about council tax valuation go to: www.voa.gov.uk.*

4.1 Have any of the following changes been made to the whole or any part of the property (including the garden)?

(a) Building works (eg extension, loft or garage conversion, removal of internal walls). If Yes, please give details including dates of all work undertaken

☐ Yes ☐ No

(b) Change of use (eg from an office to a residence)

☐ Yes ☐ No

Year

(c) Installation of replacement windows, roof windows, roof lights, glazed doors since 1 April 2002

☐ Yes ☐ No

Year(s)

(d) Addition of a conservatory

☐ Yes ☐ No

Year

4.2 If Yes to any of the questions in 4.1 and if the work was undertaken during the seller's ownership of the property:

(a) please supply copies of the planning permissions, Building Regulations approvals and Completion Certificates, OR:

(b) if none were required, please explain why these were not required – e.g. permitted development rights applied or the work was exempt from Building Regulations:

For further information about permitted development go to: www.planningportal.gov.uk

4.3 Are any of the works disclosed in 4.1 above unfinished? If Yes, please give details

☐ Yes ☐ No

4.4 Is the seller aware of any breach of planning permission conditions or Building Regulations consent conditions, unfinished work or work that does not have all necessary consents? If Yes, please give details:

☐ Yes ☐ No

4.5 Are there any planning or building control issues to resolve? If Yes, please give details:

☐ Yes ☐ No

4.6 Have solar panels been installed? If Yes: ☐ Yes ☐ No

(a) in what year were the solar panels installed? ☐ Year

(b) are the solar panels owned outright? ☐ Yes ☐ No

c) has a long lease of the roof/air space been granted to a solar panel provider? If Yes, please supply copies of the relevant documents ☐ Yes ☐ No ☐ Enclosed ☐ To follow

4.7 Is the property or any part of it:

(a) A listed building? ☐ Yes ☐ No ☐ Not known

(b) In a conservation area? ☐ Yes ☐ No ☐ Not known

If Yes, please supply copies of any relevant documents. ☐ Enclosed ☐ To follow

4.8 Are any of the trees on the property subject to a Tree Preservation Order? ☐ Yes ☐ No ☐ Not known

If Yes:

(a) Have the terms of the Order been complied with? ☐ Yes ☐ No ☐ Not known

(b) Please supply a copy of any relevant documents. ☐ Enclosed ☐ To follow

5. Guarantees and warranties

Note to seller: Please supply all available guarantees, warranties and supporting paperwork before exchange of contracts.

Note to buyer: Some guarantees only operate to protect the person who had the work carried out or may not be valid if their terms have been breached. You may wish to contact the company to establish whether it is still trading and if so, whether the terms of the guarantee will apply to you.

5.1 Does the property benefit from any of the following guarantees or warranties? If Yes, please supply a copy.

(a) New home warranty (eg NHBC or similar) ☐ Yes ☐ No ☐ Enclosed ☐ To follow

(b) Damp proofing ☐ Yes ☐ No ☐ Enclosed ☐ To follow

(c) Timber treatment ☐ Yes ☐ No ☐ Enclosed ☐ To follow

(d) Windows, roof lights, roof windows or glazed doors ☐ Yes ☐ No ☐ Enclosed ☐ To follow

(e) Electrical work — ☐ Yes ☐ No ☐ Enclosed ☐ To follow

(f) Roofing — ☐ Yes ☐ No ☐ Enclosed ☐ To follow

(g) Central heating — ☐ Yes ☐ No ☐ Enclosed ☐ To follow

(h) underpinning — ☐ Yes ☐ No ☐ Enclosed ☐ To follow

(i) Other (please state) — ☐ Enclosed ☐ To follow

5.2 Have any claims been made under any of these guarantees or warranties? If Yes, please give details — ☐ Yes ☐ No

6 Insurance

6.1 Does the seller insure the property? — ☐ Yes ☐ No

6.2 Has any buildings insurance taken out by the seller ever been:

(a) Subject to an abnormal rise in premiums? — ☐ Yes ☐ No

(b) Subject to high excesses? — ☐ Yes ☐ No

(c) Subject to unusual conditions? — ☐ Yes ☐ No

(d) Refused? — ☐ Yes ☐ No

If Yes, please give details:

6.3 Has the seller made any buildings insurance claims? If Yes, please give details: — ☐ Yes ☐ No

7 Environmental matters

Flooding

Note: Flooding may take a variety of forms: it may be seasonal or irregular or simply a one-off occurrence. The property does not need to be near a sea or river for flooding to occur. *For further information about flooding go to: www.defra.gov.uk.*

7.1 Has any part of the property (whether buildings or surrounding garden or land) ever been flooded? If Yes, please state when the flooding occurred and identify the parts that flooded:

☐ Yes ☐ No (go to 7.3)

7.2 What type of flooding occurred?

(a)	Ground water	☐ Yes	☐ No
(b)	Sewer flooding	☐ Yes	☐ No
(c)	Surface water	☐ Yes	☐ No
(d)	Coastal flooding	☐ Yes	☐ No
(e)	River flooding	☐ Yes	☐ No
(f)	Other (please state):	☐ Yes	☐ No

7.3 Has a Flood Risk Report been prepared? If Yes, please supply a copy.

☐ Yes ☐ No
☐ Enclosed ☐ To follow

For further information about the types of flooding and Flood Risk Reports go to: www.environment-agency.gov.uk.

Radon

Note: Radon is a naturally occurring inert radioactive gas found in the ground. Some parts of England and Wales are more adversely affected by it than others. Remedial action is advised for properties with a test result above the "recommended action level". *For further information about Radon go to: www.hpa.org.uk.*

7.4 Has a Radon test been carried out on the property? If Yes: ☐ Yes ☐ No

(a) Please supply a copy of the report ☐ Enclosed ☐ To follow

(b) Was the test result below the "recommended action level"? ☐ Yes ☐ No

7.5 Were any remedial measures undertaken on construction to reduce Radon gas levels in the property? ☐ Yes ☐ No Not Known

Energy Efficiency

Note: An Energy Performance Certificate (EPC) is a document that gives information about a property's energy usage. *For further information about EPCs go to www.gov.uk.*

7.6 Please supply a copy of the EPC for the property

☐ Enclosed ☐ To follow
☐ Already supplied

7.7 Have any installations in the property been financed under the Green Deal scheme? If Yes, please give details of all installations and supply a copy of your last electricity bill.

☐ Yes ☐ No
☐ Enclosed ☐ To follow

For further information about the Green Deal go to: www.gov.uk/decc.

Japanese knotweed

Note: Japanese knotweed is an invasive plan that can cause damage to property. It can take several years to eradicate.

7.8 Is the property affected by Japanese knotweed?

☐ Yes ☐ No
☐ Not known

If Yes, please state whether there is a Japanese knotweed management plan in place and supply a copy

☐ Yes ☐ No
☐ Not known
☐ Enclosed ☐ To follow

8 Rights and informal arrangements

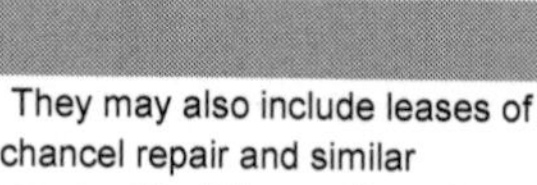

Note: Rights and arrangements may relate to access or shared use. They may also include leases of less than seven years, rights to mines and minerals, manorial rights, chancel repair and similar matters. If you are uncertain about whether a right or arrangement is covered by this question, please ask your conveyancer.

8.1 Does ownership of the property carry a responsibility to contribute towards the cost of any jointly used services, such as maintenance of a private road, a shared driveway, a boundary or drain? If Yes, please give details:

☐ Yes ☐ No

8.2 Does the property benefit from any rights or arrangements over any neighbouring property? If Yes, please give details:

☐ Yes ☐ No

8.3 Has anyone taken steps to prevent access to the property, or to complain about or demand payment for access to the property? If Yes, please give details:

☐ Yes ☐ No

8.4 Does the seller know of any of the following rights or arrangements affecting the property:

(a)	Rights of light	☐ Yes	☐ No
(b)	Rights of support from adjoining properties	☐ Yes	☐ No
c)	Customary rights (eg rights deriving from local traditions)	☐ Yes	☐ No
(d)	Other people's rights to mines and minerals under the land	☐ Yes	☐ No
e)	Chancel repair liability	☐ Yes	☐ No
(f)	Other people's rights to take things from the land (such as timber, hay or fish)	☐ Yes	☐ No

If Yes, please give details:

8.5 Are there any other rights or arrangements affecting the property? If Yes, please give details:

☐ Yes ☐ No

Services crossing the property or neighbouring property

8.6 Do any drains, pipes or wires serving the property cross any neighbour's property?

☐ Yes ☐ No ☐ Not known

8.7 Do any drains, pipes or wires leading to any neighbour's property cross the property?

☐ Yes ☐ No ☐ Not known

8.8 Is there any agreement or arrangement about drains, pipes or wires?

☐ Yes ☐ No ☐ Not known

If Yes, please supply a copy or give details:

☐ Enclosed ☐ To follow

9 Parking

9.1 What are the parking arrangements at the property?

9.2 Is the property in a controlled parking zone or within a local authority parking scheme?

☐ Yes ☐ No ☐ Not known

10 Other charges

Note: If the property is leasehold, details of lease expenses such as service charges and ground rent should be set out on the separate Leasehold Information Form. If the property is freehold, there may still be charges; for example, payments to a management company or for the use of a private drainage system.

10.1 Does the seller have to pay any charges relating to the property (excluding any payments such as council tax, utility charges etc). If Yes, please give details

☐ Yes ☐ No

11 Occupiers

11.1 Does the seller live at the property?

☐ Yes ☐ No

11.2 Does anyone else, aged 17 or over, live at the property?

☐ Yes ☐ No **Go to section 12**

11.3 Please give the full names of any occupiers (other than the seller) aged 17 or over:

11.4 Are any of the people named in 11.3 tenants or lodgers?

☐ Yes ☐ No

11.5 Is the property being sold with vacant possession?

☐ Yes ☐ No

If Yes, have all the occupiers aged 17 or over:

(a) Agreed to leave prior to completion?

☐ Yes ☐ No

(b) Agreed to sign the sale contract? If No, please supply other evidence that the property will be vacant on completion.

☐ Yes ☐ No ☐ Enclosed ☐ To follow

12 Services

Note: If the seller does not have a certificate requested below this can be obtained from the relevant Competent Persons Scheme. *For further information about Competent Persons Schemes go to: www.gov.uk*

Electricity

12.1 Has the whole or any part of the electrical installation been tested by a qualified and registered electrician?

If Yes, please state the year it was tested and provide a copy of the test certificate.

12.2 Has the property been rewired or had any electrical installation work carried out since 1 January 2005?

If Yes, please supply one of the following:

(a) A copy of the signed BS7671 Electrical Safety Certificate

(b) The installer's Building Regulations Compliance Certificate

c) The Building Control Completion Certificate

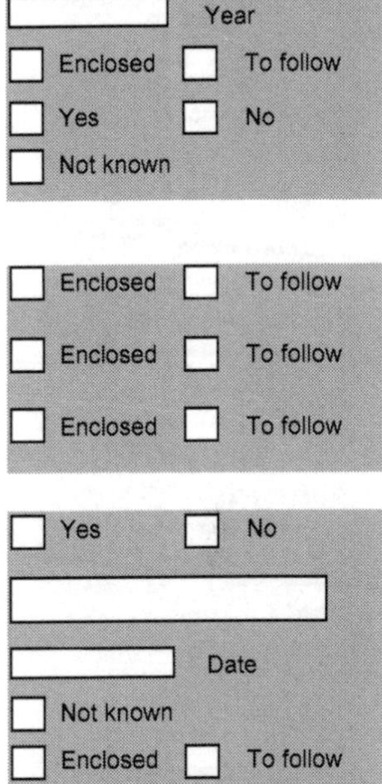

Central heating

12.3 Does the property have a central heating system? If Yes:

(a) What type of system is it (eg mains gas, liquid gas, oil, electricity, etc)?

(b) When was the heating system installed? If on or after 1 April 2005 please supply a copy of the "completion certificate" (eg CORGI or Gas Safe Register) or the "exceptional circumstances" form.

c) Is the heating system in good working order?

(d) In what year was the heating system last serviced/maintained? Please supply a copy of the inspection report.

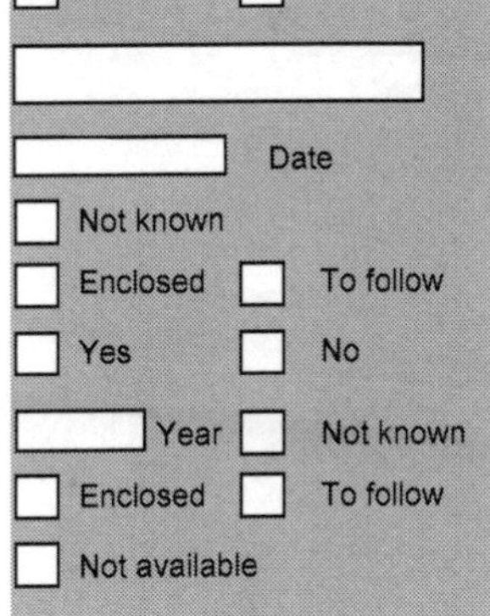

Drainage and sewerage

Note: *For further information about drainage and sewerage go to:* www.environment-agency.gov.uk .

12.4 Is the property connected to mains:

(a) Foul water drainage?

(b) Surface water drainage?

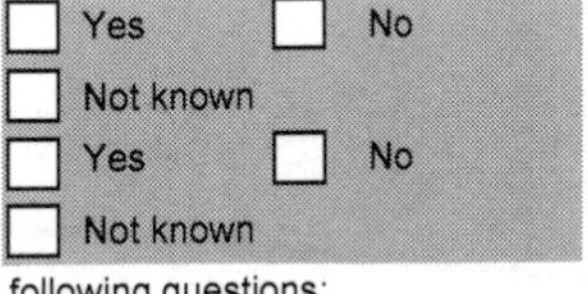

If Yes to both questions, go to section 13. If No, please answer the following questions:

12.5 Is sewerage for the property provided by:

(a) A septic tank? Yes No

(b) A sewage treatment plant? Yes No

(c) Cesspool? Yes No

12.6	Is the use of the septic tank, sewage treatment plant or cesspool shared with other properties? If Yes, how many properties share the system?	☐ Yes ☐ No ☐ Properties share
12.7	When was the system last emptied?	☐ Year
12.8	If the Property is served by a sewage treatment plant, when was the treatment plant last serviced?	☐ Year
12.9	When was the system installed?	☐ Year

Note: Some systems installed after 1 January 1991 require Buildings Regulations approval, environmental permits or registration. *For further information about permits and registration go to:* www.environment-agency.gov.uk

12.10	Is any part of the septic tank, sewage treatment plant (including any soakaway or outfall) or cesspool, or the access to it, outside the boundary of the property? If Yes, please supply a plan showing the location of the system and how access is obtained.	☐ Yes ☐ No ☐ Enclosed ☐ To follow

13 Connection to utilities and services

Please mark the Yes or No boxes to show which of the following utilities and services are connected to the property and give details of any providers.

Mains electricity ☐ Yes ☐ No	**Mains gas** ☐ Yes ☐ No
Providers' name	Provider's name
Location of meter	Location of meter
Mains water ☐ Yes ☐ No	**Mains sewerage** ☐ Yes ☐ No
Providers' name	Provider's name
Location of stopcock	
Location of meter, if any	
Telephone ☐ Yes ☐ No	**Cable** ☐ Yes ☐ No
Providers' name	Provider's name

14 Transaction information

14.1	Is this sale dependent on the seller completing the purchase of another property on the same day?	☐ Yes ☐ No

14.2 Does the seller have any special requirements about a moving date? If Yes, please give details: ☐ Yes ☐ No

14.3 Does the sale price exceed the amount necessary to repay all mortgages and charges secured on the property? ☐ Yes ☐ No

14.4 Will the seller ensure that:

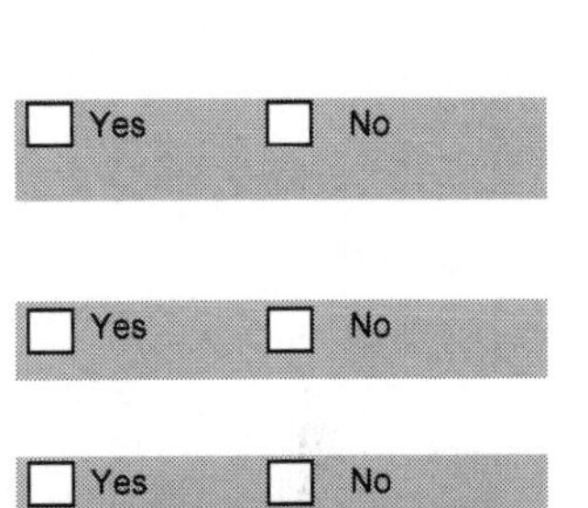

(a) All rubbish is removed from the property (including from the loft, garden, outbuildings, garages and sheds) and that the property will be left in a clean and tidy condition? ☐ Yes ☐ No

(b) If light fittings are removed, the fittings will be replaced with ceiling rose, flex, bulb holder and bulb? ☐ Yes ☐ No

(c) Reasonable care will be taken when removing any other fittings or contents ☐ Yes ☐ No

(d) Keys to all windows and doors and details of alarm codes will be left at the property or with the estate agent? ☐ Yes ☐ No

Signed.. Dated................................

Signed.. Dated................................

All sellers should sign this form

Leasehold Information Form (2nd edition) TA7

Address of the Property

Full names of the seller

Seller's Solicitor

Name of Solicitors firm

Address

Email

Reference Number

Definitions

- 'Seller' means all sellers together where the property is owned by more than one person
- 'Buyer' means all buyers together where the property is being bought by more than one person
- 'Property' means the leasehold property being sold
- 'Building' means the building containing the property
- 'Neighbour' means those occupying flats in the building

Instructions to the seller

The seller should provide all relevant documentation relating to the lease when they return this completed form to their solicitor. This may include documents given to the seller when they purchased the property, or documents subsequently given to the seller by those managing the property.

Instructions to the seller And the buyer

Please read the notes on *TA6 Property Information Form*

1 The property

1.1	What type of leasehold property does the seller own? ('Flat' includes maisonette and apartment).	☐ Flat ☐ Shared ownership ☐ Long leasehold house
1.2	Does the seller pay rent for the property? If Yes:	☐ Yes ☐ No
	(a) How much is the current yearly rent?	☐ £
	(b) How regularly is the rent paid (e.g. yearly)?	☐ Payments

2 Relevant documents

2.1	Please supply a copy of:	
	(a) the lease and any supplemental deeds	☐ Enclosed ☐ To follow ☐ Already supplied
	(b) any regulations made by the landlord or by the tenants' management company additional to those in the lease	☐ Enclosed ☐ To follow ☐ Not applicable
2.2	Please supply a copy of any correspondence from the landlord, the management company and the managing agent.	☐ Enclosed ☐ To follow
2.3	Please supply a copy of any invoices or demands and any statements and receipts for the payment of:	
	(a) maintenance or service charges for the last three years	☐ Enclosed ☐ To follow ☐ Not applicable
	(b) ground rent for the last three years	☐ Enclosed ☐ To follow ☐ Not applicable
2.4	Please supply a copy of the buildings insurance policy:	
	(a) arranged by the seller and a receipt for payment of the last premium, **or**	☐ Enclosed ☐ To follow
	(b) arranged by the landlord or management company and the schedule for the current year	☐ Enclosed ☐ To follow
2.5	Have the tenants formed a management company to manage the building? If Yes, please supply a copy of:	☐ Yes ☐ No
	(a) the Memorandum and Articles of Association	☐ Enclosed ☐ To follow
	(b) the share or membership certificate	☐ Enclosed ☐ To follow
	(c) the company accounts for the past three years	☐ Enclosed ☐ To follow

3 Management of the building

3.1	Does the landlord employ a managing agent to collect rent or manage the building?	☐ Yes ☐ No
3.2	Has any management company formed by the tenants been dissolved or struck off the register at Companies House?	☐ Yes ☐ No ☐ Not known
3.3	Do the tenants pass day-to-day responsibility for the management of the building to managing agents?	☐ Yes ☐ No

4 Contact details

4.1 Please supply contact details for the following, where appropriate. (The landlord may be, for example, a private individual, a housing association, or a management company owned by the residents. A managing agent may be employed by the landlord or by the tenants' management company to collect the rent and/or manage the building.)

	Landlord	**Managing agent contracted by the landlord**
Name		
Address		
Tel		
Email		

	Managing agent contracted by the tenants' management company
Name	
Address	
Tel	
Email	

5 Maintenance and service charges

5.1 Who is responsible for arranging the buildings insurance on the property?

☐ Seller
☐ Management company
☐ Landlord

5.2 In what year was the outside of the building last decorated?

☐ Year ☐ Not known

5.3 In what year were any internal communal parts last decorated?

☐ Year ☐ Not known

5.4 Does the seller contribute to the cost of maintaining the building?

☐ Yes ☐ No

If No to question 5.4, please continue to section 6 'Notices' and do not answer questions 5.5–5.9 below.

5.5 Does the seller know of any expense (e.g. the cost of redecoration of outside or communal areas not usually incurred annually) likely to be shown in the service charge accounts within the next three years? If Yes, please give details:

☐ Yes ☐ No

5.6 Does the seller know of any problems in the last three years regarding the level of service charges or with the management? If Yes, please give details:

☐ Yes ☐ No

5.7 Has the seller challenged the service charge or any expense in the last three years? If Yes, please give details:

☐ Yes ☐ No

5.8 Is the seller aware of any difficulties encountered in collecting the service charges from other flat owners? If Yes, please give details:

☐ Yes ☐ No

5.9 Does the seller owe any service charges, rent, insurance premium or other financial contribution? If Yes, please give details:

☐ Yes ☐ No

6 Notices

Note: A notice may be in a printed form or in the form of a letter.

6.1 Has the seller received a notice that the landlord wants to sell the building? If Yes, please supply a copy.

☐ Yes ☐ No
☐ Enclosed ☐ To follow
☐ Lost

6.2 Has the seller received any other notice about the building, its use, its condition or its repair and maintenance? If Yes, please supply a copy.

☐ Yes ☐ No
☐ Enclosed ☐ To follow
☐ Lost

7 Consents

Note: A consent may be given in a formal document, a letter or orally.

7.1 Is the seller aware of any changes in the terms of the lease or of the landlord giving any consents under the lease? If Yes, please supply a copy or, if not in writing, please give details:

☐ Yes ☐ No
☐ Enclosed ☐ To follow
☐ Lost

8 Complaints

8.1 Has the seller received any complaint from the landlord, the management company or any neighbour about anything the seller has or has not done? If Yes, please give details:

☐ Yes ☐ No

8.2 Has the seller complained or had cause to complain to or about the landlord, the management company, or any neighbour? If Yes, please give details:

☐ Yes ☐ No

9 Alterations

9.1 Is the seller aware of any alterations having been made to the property since the lease was originally granted?

☐ Yes ☐ No

If No, please go to section 10 'Enfranchisement' and do not answer 9.2 and 9.3 below.

9.2 Please give details of these alterations:

9.3 Was the landlord's consent for the alterations obtained? If Yes, please supply a copy.

☐ Yes ☐ No
☐ Not known ☐ Not required
☐ Enclosed ☐ To follow

10 Enfranchisement

Note: 'Enfranchisement' is the right of a tenant to purchase the freehold from their landlord and the right of the tenant to extend the term of the lease.

10.1 Has the seller owned the property for at least two years?

☐ Yes ☐ No

10.2 Has the seller served on the landlord a formal notice stating the seller's wish to buy the freehold or be granted an extended lease? If Yes, please supply a copy.

☐ Yes ☐ No
☐ Enclosed ☐ To follow
☐ Lost

10.3 Is the seller aware of the service of any notice relating to the possible collective purchase of the freehold of the building or part of it by a group of tenants? If Yes, please supply a copy.

☐ Yes ☐ No
☐ Enclosed ☐ To follow
☐ Lost

10.4 Is the seller aware of any response to a notice disclosed in replies to 10.2 and 10.3 above? If Yes, please supply a copy.

☐ Yes ☐ No
☐ Enclosed ☐ To follow
☐ Lost

Signed: .... Dated: ....

Each seller should sign this form.

Fittings and Contents Form

Address of the property	
Full names of the seller	

Seller's conveyancer

Name of firm	
Address	
Email	
Reference	

This form is completed by the seller to supply detailed information and documents which may be relied upon for the conveyancing process. It is important that sellers and buyers read the notes below.

Definitions

"Seller" means all sellers together if the property is owned by more than one person

"Buyer" means all buyers together if the property is being bought by more than one person.

Instructions to the Seller

This form must be completed accurately by the seller, who should check through all answers before signing it. It may become part of the contract between the seller and the buyer.

The seller should indicate clearly what is included in the sale of the property by marking each box on this form

- With a tick
- A question mark if not decided or for discussion
- If the item is excluded, the seller may insert a price for the item. The buyer can then decide whether to accept the seller's offer to sell the item. The seller and buyer should inform their conveyancers of any arrangements made about items offered for sale in this way.

If an item is offered for sale, it is the seller's responsibility to negotiate the sale with the buyer directly, or through their estate agent (if applicable). If the conveyancer is instructed to act in the negotiation, the costs of so doing may not be included in the original quote and may be subject to additional charges.

If the seller removes any fixtures, fittings or contents, the seller should be reasonably careful to ensure that any damage caused is minimised.

Unless stated otherwise, the seller will be responsible for ensuring that all rubbish is removed from the property (including from the loft, garden, outbuildings, garages and sheds), and that the property is left in a reasonably clean and tidy condition.

The buyer should check the information given by the seller in this form carefully.

1 Basic fittings

	Included	Excluded	None	Price	Comments
Boiler/immersion heater					
Radiators/wall heaters					
Night-storage heaters					
Free-standing heaters					
Gas fires (with surround)					
Electric fires (with surround)					
Light Switches					
Roof insulation					
Window fittings					
Window shutters/grilles					
Internal door fittings					
External door fittings					
Doorbell/chime					
Electric sockets					
Burglar alarm					

Other basic fittings (please state which)					

2 Television and telephone

	Included	Excluded	None	Price	Comments
Telephone receivers					
Television aerial					
Radio aerial					
Satellite dish					

3 Kitchen

Note: for each, please indicate whether the item is fitted or freestanding and whether it is included or excluded.

	Fitted	Free-standing	Included	Excluded	None	Price	Comments
Hob							
Extractor hood							
Oven/grill							
Cooker							
Microwave							
Refrigerator/fridge-freezer							
Freezer							
Dishwasher							
Tumble-dryer							
Washing machine							

4 Bathroom

	Included	Excluded	None	Price	Comments
Bath					
Shower fitting for bath					
Shower curtain					
Bathroom cabinet					
Taps					

Separate shower and fittings					
Towel rail					
Soap/toothbrush holders					
Toilet roll holders					
Bathroom mirror					

5 Carpets

	Included	Excluded	None	Price	Comments
Hall, stairs and landing					
Living room					
Dining room					
Kitchen					
Bedroom 1					
Bedroom 2					
Bedroom 3					
Other rooms (please specify)					

6 Curtains and curtain rails

	Included	Excluded	None	Price	Comments
Curtain rails/poles/pelmets					
Hall, stairs and landing					
Living room					
Dining room					
Kitchen					
Bedroom 1					
Bedroom 2					
Bedroom 3					
Other rooms (please specify)					

Curtains/blinds					
Hall, stairs and landing					
Living room					
Dining room					
Kitchen					
Bedroom 1					
Bedroom 2					
Bedroom 3					
Other rooms (please specify)					

7 Light fittings

	Included	Excluded	None	Price	Comments
Hall, stairs and landing					
Living room					
Dining room					
Kitchen					
Bedroom 1					
Bedroom 2					
Bedroom 3					
Other rooms (please specify)					

If the seller removes a light fitting, it is assumed that the seller will replace the fitting with a ceiling rose, a flex, bulb holder and bulb and that they will be left in a safe condition.

8 Fitted units

(For example: fitted cupboards, fitted shelves and fitted wardrobes)

	Included	Excluded	None	Price	Comments
Hall, stairs and landing					
Living room					
Dining room					
Kitchen					

Bedroom 1					
Bedroom 2					
Bedroom 3					
Other rooms (please specify)					

9 Outdoor area

	Included	Excluded	None	Price	Comments
Garden furniture					
Garden ornaments					
Trees, plants, shrubs					
Barbecue					
Dustbins					
Garden shed					
Greenhouse					
Outdoor heater					
Outside lights					
Water butt					
Clothes line					
Rotary line					
Other items					

10 Stock of fuel

	Included	Excluded	None	Price	Comments
Oil					
Wood					
Bottled gas					
LPG					

11 Other items

	Included	Excluded	None	Price	Comments

Signed.. Dated.................................

Signed.. Dated..................................

All sellers should sign this form

Land Registry
Transfer of whole of registered title(s)

TR1

If you need more room than is provided for in a panel, and your software allows, you can expand any panel in the form. Alternatively use continuation sheet CS and attach it to this form.

Leave blank if not yet registered.	1 Title number(s) of the property:
Insert address including postcode (if any) or other description of the property, for example 'land adjoining 2 Acacia Avenue'.	2 Property:
	3 Date:
Give full name(s). Complete as appropriate where the transferor is a company.	4 Transferor: <u>For UK incorporated companies/LLPs</u> Registered number of company or limited liability partnership including any prefix: <u>For overseas companies</u> (a) Territory of incorporation: (b) Registered number in England and Wales including any prefix:
Give full name(s). Complete as appropriate where the transferee is a company. Also, for an overseas company, unless an arrangement with Land Registry exists, lodge either a certificate in Form 7 in Schedule 3 to the Land Registration Rules 2003 or a certified copy of the constitution in English or Welsh, or other evidence permitted by rule 183 of the Land Registration Rules 2003.	5 Transferee for entry in the register: <u>For UK incorporated companies/LLPs</u> Registered number of company or limited liability partnership including any prefix: <u>For overseas companies</u> (a) Territory of incorporation: (b) Registered number in England and Wales including any prefix:
Each transferee may give up to three addresses for service, one of which must be a postal address whether or not in the UK (including the postcode, if any). The others can be any combination of a postal address, a UK DX box number or an electronic address.	6 Transferee's intended address(es) for service for entry in the register:
	7 The transferor transfers the property to the transferee

Place 'X' in the appropriate box. State the currency unit if other than sterling. If none of the boxes apply, insert an appropriate memorandum in panel 11.

8 Consideration

☐ The transferor has received from the transferee for the property the following sum (in words and figures):

☐ The transfer is not for money or anything that has a monetary value

☐ Insert other receipt as appropriate:

Place 'X' in any box that applies.

Add any modifications.

9 The transferor transfers with

☐ full title guarantee

☐ limited title guarantee

Where the transferee is more than one person, place 'X' in the appropriate box.

Complete as necessary.

10 Declaration of trust. The transferee is more than one person and

☐ they are to hold the property on trust for themselves as joint tenants

☐ they are to hold the property on trust for themselves as tenants in common in equal shares

☐ they are to hold the property on trust:

Insert here any required or permitted statement, certificate or application and any agreed covenants, declarations and so on.

11 Additional provisions

The transferor must execute this transfer as a deed using the space opposite. If there is more than one transferor, all must execute. Forms of execution are given in Schedule 9 to the Land Registration Rules 2003. If the transfer contains transferee's covenants or declarations or contains an application by the transferee (such as for a restriction), it must also be executed by the transferee.

WARNING
If you dishonestly enter information or make a statement that you know is, or might be, untrue or misleading, and intend by doing so to make a gain for yourself or another person, or to cause loss or the risk of loss to another person, you may commit the offence of fraud under section 1 of the Fraud Act 2006, the maximum penalty for which is 10 years' imprisonment or an unlimited fine, or both.

Failure to complete this form with proper care may result in a loss of protection under the Land Registration Act 2002 if, as a result, a mistake is made in the register.

Under section 66 of the Land Registration Act 2002 most documents (including this form) kept by the registrar relating to an application to the registrar or referred to in the register are open to public inspection and copying. If you believe a document contains prejudicial information, you may apply for that part of the document to be made exempt using Form EX1, under rule 136 of the Land Registration Rules 2003.

© Crown copyright (ref: LR/SC14) 07/08

Index

**